The GOLDEN KING

THE WORLD OF TUTANKHAMUN

THE GOLDEN KING

THE WORLD OF TUTANKHAMUN

Zahi Hawass

NATIONAL GEOGRAPHIC

WASHINGTON, D.C.

First published in Egypt in 2004 by
The American University in Cairo Press
113 Sharia Kasr el Aini, Cairo, Egypt
420 Fifth Avenue, New York, NY 10018
www.aucpress.com

Dar el Kutub No. 16146/03
ISBN 977 424 836 8

Design by
Andrea El-Akshar/AUC Press Design Center

Printed in Egypt

Photographic credits
Archivio White Star 84; Egypt Historical Archive 100, 105,
114, 135, 147; Kenneth Garrett i, 9, 17, 21, 40, 44, 52–53,
59, 60, 62–63, 70–71, 72, 75, 77, 78–79, 80–81, 82, 87,
116–117, 125, 126, 131, 132, 136, 144, 150–151, 152, 155,
160, 161, 162, 163; Zahi Hawass Collection 8, 13, 27, 30,
103, 137, 149; Araldo De Luca/Archivio White Star 4–5, 22,
47, 50, 88, 128; Guy W. Midkiff 37, 39; Patti Rabbit 48;
Margaret Sears 25; Supreme Council of Antiquities 109, 110,
111, 112–113, 130, 140, 143, 156, 158; Andreas F.
Voegelin/Antikenmuseum Basel iii, v, 2, 6, 10, 18, 19, 24, 26,
29, 34, 35, 54, 55, 57, 65, 66, 69, 93, 94, 97, 98, 99, 106,
118, 119, 120, 123, 124, 139, 166; Milan Zemina 14, 15, 33,
43, 90–91, 145.

Founded in 1888, the National Geographic Society is one
of the largest nonprofit scientific and educational organiza-
tions in the world. It reaches more than 285 million people
worldwide each month through its official journal,
NATIONAL GEOGRAPHIC, and its four other magazines; the
National Geographic Channel; television documentaries;
radio programs; films; books; videos and DVDs; maps;
and interactive media. National Geographic has funded
more than 8,000 scientific research projects and supports
an education program combating geographic illiteracy.

For more information, please call 1-800-NGS LINE (647-
5463) or write to the following address:

National Geographic Society
1145 17th Street N.W.
Washington, D.C. 20036-4688 U.S.A.

Log on to nationalgeographic.com; AOL Keyword:
NatGeo.

Page i and page 166:
**Canopic coffinette
of Tutankhamun**

Page ii:
**Funerary Mask of
Tutankhamun**

Page iv:
**Shabti of
Tutankhamun**

CONTENTS

THE GOLDEN AGE

In 1922, the history of Egyptology was changed forever by the discovery of the tomb of Tutankhamun. For ten years, the world watched in amazement as spectacular artifacts created during the Golden Age of Empire (c. 1550 to 1327 B.C.) poured from the tightly-packed chambers of this long-hidden royal burial. Over the decades since the tomb's discovery, millions of visitors have flocked to see these treasures at their permanent home in the Egyptian Museum. A selection of pieces left the country for the first time in 1961, and for the next fifteen years, traveling exhibits brought Tutankh-amun to the world. Thousands of people stood in line for hours to view these incomparable artifacts—the massive golden mask that covered the king's head; the solid gold coffins that contained his mummy, the jewels, the chariots, the boxes, the alabaster vases—each object more magnificent than the last. The serene beauty of the young king's face has captured the hearts of all who have seen him, and the elegance and exquisite craftsmanship of his belongings have elicited awe and admiration around the world.

Who was this young king whose golden treasures have fascinated the world for eight decades? In an ironic twist of fate, Tutankhamun's tomb escaped the scavengers of the dead—the men who plundered the royal burials that came

OPPOSITE: **Mannequin of Tutankhamun**

before and after him—because he was deliberately wiped from the pages of history by his successors. In fact, Tutankhamun was a relatively minor king who ruled for only a decade and died before the age of twenty. He lived during a fascinating period in Egyptian history, when the world was changing rapidly and Egypt could no longer remain isolated and aloof.

The objects illustrated in this book tell the story of the height of the Golden Age, an era when Egypt's foreign possessions were secure and her borders safe, when gold poured into her coffers and her kings married the daughters of their old enemies instead of confronting them on the battlefield. At this moment—the apex of the empire—a rogue player stepped onto the stage. This was Akhenaten, the heretic king, seen by some as a saint and by others as a monster. His wife was the beautiful Nefertiti, and Tutankhamun may have been his son.

The epilogue of this book is dedicated to six objects from Tutankhamun's tomb that will be new to most people. They have been hidden away in the basement of the Egyptian Museum in Cairo, where they were stored after being taken from the tomb. They were recorded by the tomb's discoverer, Howard Carter and published in a scholarly tome, but are known only to Egyptologists. Here, in luminous photographs by Kenneth Garrett, they make their debut, as they are brought for the first time to the attention of the public.

Tutankhamun became king in the waning years of a great religious revolution inaugurated by Akhenaten. He was only a child when he was raised to the throne of the Two Lands, and had barely gained his young manhood when he died. The objects found in his tomb help to illuminate his short life, but, as Howard Carter, the man who discovered his tomb, observed, "The mystery of his life still eludes us—the shadows move but the dark is never quite dispersed." In order to understand the golden boy-king, we must go back several centuries, to the time of the great warrior kings who built an empire.

Ointment jar The lion figure on the lid of this calcite jar carries the cartouche of Tutankhamun. Hunting scenes adorn the sides. **FOLLOWING PAGES: Golden shrine of Tutankhamun**

CHAPTER ONE

BUILDING AN EMPIRE

THE GREAT DYNASTY TO WHICH TUTANKHAMUN WAS HEIR rose from the ashes of the Middle Kingdom (c. 2055–1650 B.C.), a time of great peace, security, and centralized authority. Egypt had made its first attempts to expand its borders during this period, erecting fortresses in Nubia, the land to the south. During the late Twelfth and Thirteenth Dynasties, there had been an influx of foreigners from western Asia into the Delta. As the power of the central government began to wane, these settlers took control, first of the eastern Delta, and then of most of Egypt. They ruled as the Fifteenth Dynasty from their northern stronghold of Avaris, and were called the Hekau Khasut, or Hyksos in Greek—'rulers of foreign lands.' The Nubian territory once controlled by the Twelfth Dynasty kings became part of the kingdom of Kush, based far to the south near the third cataract, at the site of Kerma.

By 1580, a native dynasty, the Seventeenth, had come to power in the Theban region, evidently as vassals to the Hyksos. The eighth king of this dynasty, Seqenenre Taa II, initiated a military campaign to oust the foreign invaders. The skull of his mummy bears the marks of Asiatic battle-axes, testimony that he almost certainly died in battle. His mother, Tetisheri, was the first in a long line of extremely powerful queens, and lived long after the deaths of her husband and her son. Seqenenre Taa II was married to Ahhotep, with whom he had at least two sons. The elder, Kamose, continued the war with the Hyksos after his father was killed. A stela from the reign of

OPPOSITE: **Statue of Thutmosis III** Tuthmosis III came to the throne as a child, and grew up in the shadow of his stepmother and aunt, Hatshepsut. When he became sole pharaoh, he was probably in his twenties, at the height of his youth and strength.

Stele of Tetisheri
The upper part of this stele from Abydos shows King Ahmose making offerings to his grandmother; the text below details provisions for her cult at this important site, burial place of Osiris.

this king tells of the capture of a spy carrying messages between the Hyksos and the kings of Kush to the south, who were planning to unite and crush the Thebans between them. Kamose disappears from the historical record after a short time, and may also have been a casualty of war.

When Kamose died, after a reign of only about five years, he was succeeded by his much younger brother, Ahmose. For the first years of the new king's rule, the reins of power were held firmly by his mother, Ahhotep. This strong queen kept the army ready for her son, and perhaps even led some military sorties against the Hyksos herself. When he reached his majority, Ahmose continued the great war of independence, and succeeded in driving the hated invaders from the shores of Egypt. The tomb inscription of one of Ahmose's generals, a man named Ahmose son of Ebana, tells of this great victory and the subsequent siege by the Egyptians of a Hyksos fortress called Sharuhen in southern Palestine. Ahmose also mounted campaigns south into Nubia, doing battle with the army of the Kushite king. The seed of empire was planted during his reign, to come to fruition several generations later.

Ahmose built monuments all over Egypt, from the Hyksos stronghold of Avaris in the north, where he may have constructed a palace on the ruins of their citadel, to Thebes in the south, where he left monuments in the Amun precinct at Karnak. The cult of Amun, originally a local god of the Theban area, had first become important in the Middle Kingdom, whose first rulers came from this region. Under Ahmose and his successors Amun became the preeminent state god, and his temple at Karnak grew.

OPPOSITE: **Sarcophagus of Queen Ahhotep** This gilded wooden sarcophagus was found in the burial of Ahhotep, mother of kings Kamose and Ahmose, on the west bank at Thebes, along with a number of treasures. Included in these were golden flies, usually awarded for military valor.

At Abydos, one of the most ancient sacred sites in Egypt and mystical home of the great god of the underworld, Osiris, Ahmose built the last known pyramid complex in ancient Egypt. The temple in this complex was decorated with reliefs depicting battles between Egyptians and Asiatics, most likely celebrating the victory of the Thebans over their Hyksos foes. He also left monuments celebrating his grandmother, Tetisheri. Ahmose was married to his sister, Ahmose-Nefertari, who also had a cult structure of some sort, perhaps a subsidiary pyramid, at Abydos. It is likely that Ahmose also built at Memphis, traditional administrative center of Egypt and home to the cult of an important creator god named Ptah.

Ahmose and his queen Ahmose-Nefertari had several sons. The eldest, crown-prince to his father, died young, and the second son, Amenhotep (I) became heir to the throne. He may have served as coregent during his father's lifetime, although he was probably still a child at the time of his father's death.

From at least the time of Seqenenre Taa II and Ahhotep, princesses of the Seventeenth and Eighteenth Dynasty only marry kings, thus concentrating the family's power and wealth within a closed circle. The king was theoretically the son of Amun, and an important role played by the royal women of the Eighteenth Dynasty was 'god's wife of Amun.' The holders of this title seem to have wielded significant power independent of the king. Ahmose-Nefertari, who was the first to hold this title, was extremely important during her son's reign.

ABOVE: **Divine triad** In the center of this calcite statue is Amun-Re, principal state god for most of the New Kingdom. He is flanked by Thutmosis I and his queen, Ahmose. This statue was originally carved during the early New Kingdom, damaged (perhaps in the reign of Akhenaten), and reworked in the reign of Tutankhamun.

She probably served as her son's regent during his early years, and outlived him, remaining 'god's wife of Amun' into the reign of his successor.

Amenhotep I continued the military campaigns begun by his father. His most successful campaigns were to the south, where he fought against the Nubians, setting the stage for the Egyptian empire that would soon follow. The story of these campaigns, carried out in the eighth and ninth years of his reign, is told in the tombs of Ahmose son of Ebana and Ahmose Pennekhbet, soldiers who went south with the young pharaoh. These two men would themselves have been very young at the time, as they lived on into the reigns of Ahmose's heirs. The successful Nubian wars brought in gold and luxury items to replenish the coffers of the kingdom, and the empire was born.

During a reign of about twenty years, Amenhotep I opened or reopened a number of quarries and mines in order to provide materials for his many building projects. In the Theban area, he erected a chapel in Karnak and bark stations (places where the sacred boat of the gods could rest during their festival journeys) at Deir al-Bahari and Dra Abu-Naga (where the kings of the Seventeenth Dynasty were buried). At Abydos, he finished the decoration of Ahmose's pyramid temple and also built a chapel dedicated to his father; at various sites in the south, including Elephantine and Sai Island, he built monuments for himself and his mother. We do not know for sure where this king was buried: a tomb in the Valley of the King's has tentatively been labeled as his, but with little evidence; a Polish archaeologist is sure that he will find it at Deir al-Bahari. Many Egyptologists believe that a tomb found in the 1990s by German archaeologist Daniel Polz at Dra Abu-Naga is the tomb of Amenhotep I, but there is still no conclusive proof.

Amenhotep I did not produce any sons, at least none that can be identified with certainty by scholars. We know of one queen, Meritamun, but she is not believed to have borne any sons; another wife was named Sitkamose. A king's sister and god's wife named Sitamun is thought to have been his daughter.

The next king was Thutmosis I, whose father is unknown and whose mother was named Seniseneb; some scholars believe that he was a member of the family of the high priests of Amun. He married a princess named Ahmose, whom some scholars believe to have been a member of the family of Amenhotep I. However, others think it more likely that she was the biological sister of Thutmosis I.

Thutmosis I ruled for eleven years, pursuing the Nubian conquests initiated by his predecessors. A series of fortresses, some built originally in the Middle Kingdom, lay along the southern stretches of the Nile; the pharaohs of the Eighteenth Dynasty controlled trade along the river from these strongholds. It is likely that Thutmosis I, despite his short reign, was responsible for the final defeat of the Kingdom of Kush, the only real threat in the south to Egyptian hegemony. Under this king, who left a record of his victories on the rocks of the island of Tombos, the southern border of Egypt was extended far to the south. By the end of his reign, Nubia to the Second Cataract had become an Egyptian province. An Egyptian viceroy, known as the Mayor of the South Nome, was put in charge of this region.

Egypt's principal rival to the north was the kingdom of the Mitanni, which was in the process of building its own empire. The Mitanni are thought originally to have been Indo-Aryan nomads who settled in the northern Mesopotamian region sometime in the mid-second millennium B.C. Another Indo-Aryan kingdom based nearby, that of the Hittites, was also emerging at this time. During the early Eighteenth Dynasty, the Mitanni and the Hittites fought one another for control of what is now northern Syria, with the Mitanni first taking the lead.

In about 1525, after his successful Nubian campaign, Thutmosis I mounted an expedition to Syria to fight the Mitanni on their own ground, traveling as far as the Euphrates River. He won the battle and erected a victory stele on the shores of the river (stopping to hunt elephants on the way home), but the Mitanni remained a powerful presence in the region. In contrast to the situation in Nubia, which was now effectively a province of Egypt, vassal rulers of local blood were placed in charge of cities under Egyptian control in the regions of Palestine and Lebanon.

After his victories to south and north, Thutmosis I pulled his forces back to Egypt and focused on building projects within its borders. His most significant additions were to the temple of Amun at Karnak, where he built new pylons as well as a number of other monuments. At Abydos, he left no major monument of his own, but donated objects and statues to the cults of his predecessors there. Giza, where the cult of the Fourth Dynasty kings and the worship of the Great Sphinx as Horemakhet (Horus in the Horizon) was flourishing, also received his attention.

Overview of Karnak The most important temple to Amun was on the east bank of the river at Thebes, administrative and religious center of Upper Egypt in the New Kingdom. This sprawling complex houses monuments erected by most of the kings of this period.

The tomb of Thutmosis I is the first that we know with certainty was cut into the cliffs of the Valley of the Kings, although its exact location is still under debate. He founded the village of Deir al-Madina, where the workmen who carved and painted the great royal tombs in the Valley of the Kings lived with their families. It is possible that Amenhotep I had established the workforce that resided here; he and his mother Ahmose-Nefertari were worshipped by the craftsmen and their families throughout the New Kingdom.

Queen Ahmose bore Thutmosis I a princess named Hatshepsut, who married her half-brother, also named Thutmosis. After an eleven-year reign Thutmosis I died and was succeeded by this prince, who became Thutmosis II. He ruled for only three years and thus did not have time to leave much in the way of monuments behind him. There is evidence that he did some building at Karnak, and probably carried out at least one campaign into Nubia. Thutmosis II and Hatshepsut had at least one child, a girl named Neferure.

Thutmosis II was succeeded on the throne by a son, also called Thutmosis (the third king of that name), born to him by a minor wife named Isis. Thutmosis

The rulers of Punt Carved into the walls of her mortuary temple at Deir al-Bahari is the record of an expedition that Hatshepsut sent to Punt, thought to lie either on the Red Sea coast or in Sudan. These reliefs include details of the exotic flora and fauna encountered by the Egyptians, as well as images of the king of Punt and his wife.

III was a child at his father's death and his stepmother, who was also his aunt, acted as his regent. Hatshepsut had inherited the title of god's wife of Amun from her grandmother, Ahmose-Nefertari, and clearly held real power. Biographical texts inscribed in the tombs of several high officials of the period make it clear that she held the reigns of government tightly in her own hands from the beginning of her stepson's rule, if not before.

It was not long, between two and seven years, before Hatshepsut gave up any pretence of simply marking time for the child who officially held the throne, and took to herself the full titulary and powers of a true pharaoh. Although queens played extremely important roles, representing the major goddesses of Egypt beside their husbands, women were not, according to the precepts of the Egyptian worldview, permitted to rule the country. The king was, by definition, male. Therefore, Hatshepsut portrayed herself in the majority of her reliefs and sculptures as a man, with all the usual pharaonic regalia. She also took care, in her mortuary temple at Deir al-Bahari, to portray herself as the divine offspring of Amun and the chosen heir of her earthly father, Thutmosis I. She emphasizes her pure bloodline and descent from the line of Ahhotep and Ahmose-Nefertari (supporting the theory that her mother, Ahmose, was of this line).

Hatshepsut ruled as pharaoh for over twenty years, watching over a land of peace and prosperity. Her royal steward was a man named Senenmut, a man of apparently humble birth who seems to have been Hatshepsut's most important and trusted official. He bore many titles, and had two tombs, one of which is very close to Hatshepsut's mortuary temple. Senenmut was the

OPPOSITE: **The official Senenmut with Princess Neferure** Hatshepsut appears to have relied a great deal on Senenmut, to whom she entrusted the care and raising of her daughter Neferure. Senenmut was so honored by this king that he was permitted to hide images of himself in her mortuary temple.

tutor of Neferure, daughter of Hatshepsut and Thutmosis II, and is shown with her in a number of statues. Some have speculated that Hatshepsut and Senenmut were lovers, although there is no solid evidence for this.

With the help of Senenmut and her other high officials, Hatshepsut poured the resources of the country into ambitious building projects up and down the length of the Nile. She left monuments from Nubia far to the south to the old Hyksos capital of Avaris in the north, and everywhere in between. Much of her attention was focused on Thebes, where she added much to the temple at Karnak, including a series of monolithic granite obeslisks quarried at Aswan.

Recorded on the walls of her mortuary temple at Deir al-Bahari is an expedition to the land of Punt. This was once thought to be in Somalia, but now is thought perhaps to be on the Red Sea coast between Ethiopia and Sudan. This was an exotic land, from which the Egyptians brought back goods such as myrrh and gold. The king of Punt is depicted with his enormously fat wife and the donkey whose job it was to carry her, clearly a source of amazement for the visiting Egyptians.

In two reliefs from the twentieth year of their joint reign, Hatshepsut and Thutmosis III are depicted side by side, clearly represented as equals. Two years later, in about 1500 B.C., Hatshepsut disappears from the official historical record, and Thutmosis III emerges as the sole ruler of the Two Lands. The fate of this energetic, unique female pharaoh is unknown; she may have died, or have lived on to advise her stepson. Late in his sole reign, Thutmosis III ordered his aunt's name chiseled from her monuments, thus attempting to wipe her name from history.

Thutmosis III is remembered as a great warrior pharaoh. He may have led a military expedition into Nubia. This would probably have been a policing action, and he soon concentrated on the situation to the northeast. At the time of his accession to sole rule, there were three main powers in Syro-Palestine: a coalition of cities led by the ruler of Qadesh; the kingdom of Tunip; and the Mitanni, who controlled the land beyond the Euphrates. One of his first major campaigns was against the city of Megiddo, part of the Qadesh coalition. He won the battle by taking a dangerous but direct route through the mountains,

OPPOSITE: **Kneeling statue of Thutmosis III** This exquisite calcite statue depicts the great warrior king Thutmosis III offering jars of some liquid, perhaps wine or milk, to a god.

his army marching single-file for three days, in order to launch a surprise attack on the city. It took almost a decade, and sixteen more campaigns, to beat the enemy into permanent submission. In his thirty-third year of reign, Qadesh and Tunip were finally subdued, and the Egyptian army crossed the Euphrates into Mitanni territory. This campaign was successful, although the Mitanni remained problematic into the reigns of his successors.

During the reign of Thutmosis III, booty from both north and south flowed into the treasuries of Egypt, providing the king with enormous resources to support his ambitious building programs. He is known to have built more than fifty temples, including monuments in Syria-Palestine and Nubia. His most important monuments were in the precinct of Amun at Karnak, who had by this time been fused with the ancient sun god Re to become Amun-Re, king of the gods. Within a large temple the king built for his jubilee (a festival of renewal celebrated by long-lived pharaohs first after thirty years of rule, and at shorter intervals thereafter) are reliefs which identify him as a scholar as well as a warrior. He took scientists with him on his expeditions to record the exotic flora and fauna they encountered in their travels. They brought many things back with them, including a chicken. Also at Karnak are Annals that record the king's victories. A recently discovered inscription in the granite quarries at Aswan record that in Year 25 he sent his architect south to cut two obelisks for his father, Amun-Re of Karnak.

In the tradition of Egyptian pharaohs, Thutmosis III took several wives. He is thought to have married Hatshepsut's daughter Neferure, with whom he is not known to have had children. In addition to his Egyptian wives, this king seems to have taken several Syrian princesses into his household; the recent excavation of a small palace in the Delta decorated with Minoan frescoes suggests that he may also have had a Cretan queen. He also brought into his court foreign princes; these were to be brought up as Egyptians, thus guaranteeing their loyalty. His heir, Amenhotep II, was born to Merire-Hatshepsut, who is thought to have been non-royal.

Statue of Thutmosis III Tuthmosis III came to the throne as a child, and grew up in the shadow of his stepmother and aunt, Hatshepsut. When he became sole pharaoh, he was probably in his twenties, at the height of his youth and strength.

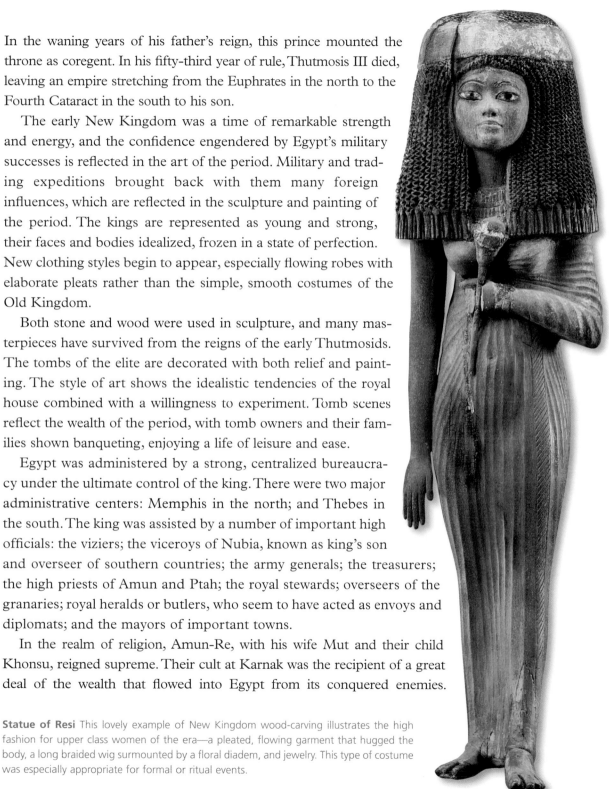

In the waning years of his father's reign, this prince mounted the throne as coregent. In his fifty-third year of rule, Thutmosis III died, leaving an empire stretching from the Euphrates in the north to the Fourth Cataract in the south to his son.

The early New Kingdom was a time of remarkable strength and energy, and the confidence engendered by Egypt's military successes is reflected in the art of the period. Military and trading expeditions brought back with them many foreign influences, which are reflected in the sculpture and painting of the period. The kings are represented as young and strong, their faces and bodies idealized, frozen in a state of perfection. New clothing styles begin to appear, especially flowing robes with elaborate pleats rather than the simple, smooth costumes of the Old Kingdom.

Both stone and wood were used in sculpture, and many masterpieces have survived from the reigns of the early Thutmosids. The tombs of the elite are decorated with both relief and painting. The style of art shows the idealistic tendencies of the royal house combined with a willingness to experiment. Tomb scenes reflect the wealth of the period, with tomb owners and their families shown banqueting, enjoying a life of leisure and ease.

Egypt was administered by a strong, centralized bureaucracy under the ultimate control of the king. There were two major administrative centers: Memphis in the north; and Thebes in the south. The king was assisted by a number of important high officials: the viziers; the viceroys of Nubia, known as king's son and overseer of southern countries; the army generals; the treasurers; the high priests of Amun and Ptah; the royal stewards; overseers of the granaries; royal heralds or butlers, who seem to have acted as envoys and diplomats; and the mayors of important towns.

In the realm of religion, Amun-Re, with his wife Mut and their child Khonsu, reigned supreme. Their cult at Karnak was the recipient of a great deal of the wealth that flowed into Egypt from its conquered enemies.

Statue of Resi This lovely example of New Kingdom wood-carving illustrates the high fashion for upper class women of the era—a pleated, flowing garment that hugged the body, a long braided wig surmounted by a floral diadem, and jewelry. This type of costume was especially appropriate for formal or ritual events.

This cult enjoyed a very close relationship with the royal house, with the kings, as we have seen, represented as divine children of the great god himself and the most important queens taking on the title of god's wife of Amun. Many other gods flourished at the same time, housed in their own local temples. Egypt, with the king on the throne and Amun-Re in the sky, moved into the second half of the second millennium a mighty power, dominating the Near East.

Our knowledge of New Kingdom religion is greatly enhanced by the decoration of the royal tombs, which included material from the Book of the Dead, more correctly called the Book of What Is in the Netherworld. The fundamental theme of these scenes and texts was the nightly journey of the sun god, Re, on whose boat the deceased king was thought to travel. Together, sun god and king passed through the twelve regions of the Nether-world or Duat, facing many dangers and bringing light to the inhabitants there. In the morning, the sun rose again on the eastern horizon, insuring that the king too would be reborn and re-enacting the moment of the first creation.

Tomb of Thutmosis III The cartouche-shaped Burial Chamber of this great king was painted with scenes from the Book of the Dead, designed to look as though a papyrus had been unrolled around the walls. The spells illustrated here would have served to aid the king in his journey through the Duat, the dangerous realm that lay beneath the horizon.

CHAPTER TWO

THE GOLDEN AGE

L IKE HIS FATHER, AMENHOTEP II WAS A WARRIOR, AND WAS proud of his prowess in the arts of the battlefield. He boasts of having once shot arrows through a target of copper while driving his own chariot. Over the course of a reign of between twenty-five and thirty-five years, he consolidated the empire built by his predecessors and ushered in a golden age of unprecedented stability and prosperity.

In his early years of rule, both as coregent to his aged father and then as sole king, Amenhotep II carried out military campaigns into Syria-Palestine that served to cement the empire carved out by his father and great-grandfather. The vassal cities that had given his father so much trouble had continued to revolt: In the first campaign of his sole rule, Amenhotep captured seven vassal rulers who had continued to rebel against their Egyptian overlords, brought them back to Egypt, and executed them. He also carried out mass deportations in both Syria and Palestine, giving notice that he would brook no challenges to his authority. He did not, however, attempt to cross the Euphrates again, and seemed content to share power with the Mitanni, whose king sent a delegation bearing tribute and seeking peace with the Egyptian king. The embassy was successful; it is likely that both empires were interested in building an alliance, with an eye on the two other great powers rising in the region: the Hittites and the Babylonians. Of these, the Hittites were to prove the most troublesome in the years to come.

Following the pattern set by his ancestors, Amenhotep II carried out building projects all over Egypt; however, most of these are fragmentary, having been dismantled,

OPPOSITE: **Statue of Amenhotep II**

built over, or reused by kings who came after him. His best-known work is a temple he constructed at Giza, dedicated to the Great Sphinx as the sun god Horemakhet (Horus in the Horizon). The Memphite desert was very important as a training ground for young princes; and the area near the Sphinx was known as the Valley of the Gazelles. The text in Amenhotep II's temple here is very interesting, as it tells the story of how, as a prince, he used to jump his horses. The courtiers were all afraid, and told his father how dangerous this was, but Thutmosis III was proud of his son, and was glad to see that his heir would be a well-trained warrior. Like all kings of this dynasty, Amenhotep II also built at Karnak.

Amenhotep II had numerous children, at least nine or ten of them male, by his wives and concubines. None of his wives, however, were granted the title of 'great royal wife'; instead, his mother, Merire-Hatshepsut, continued to play this role throughout his reign. A prince named Thutmosis, son of a woman of lesser rank named Tiaa, became the next king. There is no evidence that he was the designated crown prince, and indeed defaced mon-

Faience models
Models were important items in most tombs, as they could substitute for real materials. These four pieces—a pomegranate, a piece of fruit, and two lotus buds—come from the tomb of Amenhotep II.

uments belonging to other princes that were found in Amenhotep II's temple at Giza hint at a struggle over the succession.

As Thutmosis IV, the new pharaoh left a monumental stele between the paws of the Great Sphinx at Giza in which he tells of resting in the shadow of this massive stone creature while on a hunting trip in the near-by desert. According to this tale, as he, still only a prince, slept, the Sphinx spoke to him and asked him to clear the sand from around its body. In return for this service, the Sphinx promised him the kingship. Both prince and ancient statue appear to have kept their promises.

Thutmosis IV ruled for only eight years, but was able to accomplish a great deal. He undertook a military expedition into Syria-Palestine early in his reign, but this may have been more of an imperial procession than an actual campaign. In fact, he had little campaigning to do, having inherited a country fundamentally at peace. He sealed the Egyptian alliance with the powerful Mitanni through marriage with a daughter of their king, Artatama I.

The dream stele of Thutmosis IV
Embraced by the great paws of the Sphinx at Giza is this stele, inscribed with the story of how Tuthmosis IV cleared the sand from this colossal rock-cut statue, and was reward-ed by the god with the throne of Egypt.

It is during the reign of Thutmosis IV that the beginnings of the rise of the sun-cult can be observed. There is some evidence that this king iden-tified himself with the sun god, and may have consid-ered himself divine in his own lifetime. Statues from his reign depict him with almond-shaped eyes that lend his face an eerie, unearthly quality that may be associated with this cul-tic change. Current scholarly speculation suggests that this shift in royal dogma, which would come to fruition in the next reigns, was the result of a number of factors. The priesthood of Amun, principal god of

the Thutmosids and recipient of vast amounts of tribute, may have grown too strong for the comfort of the royal house; the rise of the sun cult is seen by some as an attempt to curb this power. Another factor may have been the growth of personal piety seen during the earlier part of the dynasty: perhaps by becoming a god himself, the king could be part of the pantheon worshiped by the populace, and thus bring power back to the royal house. The rise of the empire is another important potential factor: by becoming one with the sun, always the most important Egyptian god, the king could watch over all of the Egyptian lands from his vantage point in the sky.

In addition to his Mitanni princess, this king had a number of other wives, some of whom were raised to the status of queen. However, none of them seems to have been as important as his mother, who held the title god's wife of Amun, and was identified with the mother-goddess Mut, as well as with the goddesses Isis and Hathor. The mother of the next king, Amenhotep III, never reached the rank of queen.

THE REIGN OF THE SUN KING

Amenhotep III was born into a world where Egypt reigned supreme. Its coffers were filled with gold, and its vassals bowed down before the mighty rulers of the Two Lands. The new king was probably only a child, perhaps twelve years old, when he ascended the throne. By at least the second year of his reign, he had taken as his queen a girl named Tiye, who was not born a princess. In a significant change of policy from the reigns of his father, grandfather, and great-grandfather, Tiye immediately became 'great royal wife,' and outranked even Mutemwiya, Amenhotep III's mother.

OPPOSITE: **Thutmosis IV with his mother, Tia** The king sits here next to his mother, Tia, who is shown as equal to him in importance. Mother and son embrace one another, each with an arm around the other's body. RIGHT: **Head of Queen Tiye** Wife of Amenhotep III and mother of Akhenaten, Tiye was a woman of enormous power and influence at the Egyptian court. She was also a great beauty, as this exquisitely sculpted head here attests.

Tiye was the daughter of a master of the horse, commander of chariotry, and overseer of the cattle of Min (the god of fertility) named Yuya and his wife, Tjuya, who was a priestess of Amun, Hathor, and Min. The connection of both husband and wife with Min suggests that they hailed from Akhmim, where the Supreme Council of Antiquities has recently begun to uncover the remains of a great temple complex to this god. Some scholars have speculated that Yuya and Tjuya were of foreign birth, but there is no good evidence to substantiate this theory. Yuya also held the title of god's father, which was carried both by high officials such as the vizier, and by men of lower rank. In this case, it is thought that he received the title due to his position as the king's father-in-law. In addition to Tiye, Yuya and Tjuya are known to have had at least one son, Anen, who was the second prophet of Amun; they may also have had another son, Ay, who came to prominence later in the dynasty.

Tiye is featured prominently on her husband's monuments, and seems to have borne more real power than the queens who came before her. Her name is even written in a cartouche, like that of the king. In a private tomb from her husband's reign, she is depicted seated on a throne. This throne is decorated along the sides with the queen in the form of a sphinx trampling her enemies, the female counterpart of a motif previously applied hitherto only to kings. However, she is not always shown as the equal of the king: On a colossal statue of Amenhotep III from his mortuary temple at Thebes, Queen Tiye, with several of her daughters, is shown in the more usual diminutive size beside the legs of her husband.

Putting her non-royal origins beside her evident power, scholars have long assumed that the marriage between Amenhotep III and Tiye was a love match. However, scholars now think it possible that her parents, Yuya and Tjuya, actually held a good deal of influence in the central administration under Thutmosis IV, and may even have served as regents during the minority of the young king. The marriage may then have been a successful bid for power by an ambitious family. They were granted the unusual privilege of burial in the Valley of the Kings, where their partially plundered but still rich tomb was discovered in 1905.

OPPOSITE: **Chair of Sitamun** Amenhotep III and Tiye had a number of children. One of them, Sitamun, married her father and became a great royal wife, a position that may have been primarily religious. This wooden chair was found in the tomb of Tiye's parents, Yuya and Tjuya.

View of the palace at Malkata In the thirtieth year of his reign, Amenhotep III built a mud-brick palace on the western bank at Thebes, near the site of his enormous mortuary temple. It is likely that the royal family took up residence here when they were in the Theban area; the palace was also used for rituals involved with the king's Sed Festival.

The royal offspring of Amenhotep III and his great royal wife Tiye included at least two sons, Thutmosis and Amenhotep, and four daughters, Sitamun, Henuttaneb, Isis, and Nebetah, several of whom the king himself married. Amenhotep III had other wives, including foreign princesses: We know of two from Syrian; two from Mitanni; two from Babylon; and one from a province of southeast Asia Minor called Arzawa. Late in the reign, the royal family had a primary residence at Malkata, on the west bank of ancient Thebes, which was occupied from about the time of the king's first jubilee on. This palace has been excavated and is known to have been extensive and beautifully decorated with plastered reliefs. Although the archaeological record is silent on their other homes, we know that the other major center of power during this period was at Memphis, and it is likely that there was another major palace here. A palace found in Abu Ghorab in the Fayoum was used to house foreign queens when they became old, where they were guarded by dwarves.

Amenhotep III, with Tiye beside him, ruled Egypt for thirty-eight years. During his reign, the solar cult that had begun to flourish under Thutmosis IV became even more prominent. The sun god was a complex creature, whose dogma had been developing for thousands of years. In addition to his main incarnation as Re, this god was associated with the creator Atum as well as with deities such as Khepri, the scarab-headed god representing the morning sun, and Osiris, with whom Re merged at night. Another aspect of this god was the Aten; according to texts dating back at least to the Middle Kingdom, this was the disk of the sun, with which the king merged at death. This divine aspect, unusual in that it was not anthropomorphic, was chosen by Amenhotep III as a primary focus of his incarnation. It has been suggested that the rise of the Aten was linked specifically with maintenance of the empire, as the area over which, at least theoretically, the sun ruled. By associating himself with the visible disk of the sun, the king put himself symbolically over all of the lands where it could be seen—all of the known world, in fact.

In the thirtieth year of his reign, Amenhotep III celebrated his first Sed festival, or jubilee, from his palace at Malkata; he celebrated two more of these before his death. The Sed festival was an important event whose exact significance is still being debated. It certainly included rituals designed symbolically to rejuvenate the king and renew his hold on the throne of Egypt. It may also have celebrated that he had carried out all that the gods had asked him to do, and may have marked the moment at which his mortuary complex, both tomb and temple, were complete. There is clear evidence that at this point in his reign, Amenhotep III became not just associated with the gods of Egypt, but became their living incarnation. Many statues from the period after this jubilee show the king as various gods, including the creator gods Ptah, Re, and Atum. Two of the king's daughters were raised to the status of great royal wife, relationships modeled on those of the gods, who could marry their sisters, daughters, and even mothers. The palace at Malqata had an enormous artificial lake attached to it. Amenhotep III and Tiye took pleasure cruises on this lake in their Aten bark; these probably also had ritual significance associated with the festival.

At this point in his reign, the artistic style of the court underwent a dramatic change. Previously, royal art had followed the classical traditions of the early part of the dynasty. Forms and details were idealized and elegantly simple, the ancient canon of proportions was followed. After Year 30,

Amenhotep III is shown with a childlike face: round, large in proportion to his body, and with otherwordly, almond-shaped eyes like those seen in the late art of the reign of his father, Thutmosis IV. His attire becomes more ornate and laden with solar and funerary symbolism. His torso becomes almost chubby, his stomach shown as rounder and softer, no longer the flat, athletically muscled abdomen of the traditional king. This change in artistic style is thought to be associated with his rejuvenation and divinization.

The diplomatic correspondence of late Eighteenth Dynasty, which includes letters sent from princes of Syria-Palestine to Amenhotep III, gives a good sense of the power held by the Egyptian king. The tone of the foreign rulers is subservient, they address the king as 'My lord my god, my sun god,' and have to comply with peremptory requests from the pharaoh such as "send your daughter to the king, your lord and as presents send twenty healthy slaves, silver chariots, and healthy horses." A letter to the prince of Gezer is a request to supply forty beautiful women at a cost of forty pieces of silver for each; "so send very beautiful women in whom there is no blemish." The king continues, reassuringly, "and may you know that the king is in good health, like the sun god, and that this troops, his chariots and his horses are very well indeed, for Amun has put the Upper land and the Lower land, the rising and the setting of the sun under the feet of the king."

The eldest son of Amenhotep III and Tiye was named Thutmosis, and was designated crown prince at an early age. He was high priest of Ptah at Memphis, and assisted his father with important religious ceremonies such as the burial of the Apis bull, sacred to Ptah of Memphis. However, he died before his father, and a younger brother, named Amenhotep like his father, took his place.

There has been an enormous amount of debate about whether or not Amenhotep IV was raised to the throne before the death of his father or whether he succeeded to the throne only at the old king's death. Those who favor a coregency vote for a joint reign of anywhere from two to twelve years. Scholarly opinion has leaned toward sole rule for both kings for the last decades or so, but important recent scholarship is providing new evidence in favor of a coregency. The jury is still out.

OPPOSITE: **Statue of Amenhotep III** This life-size figure of Amenhotep III was found in 1989 in Luxor Temple, part of a cache of statuary discovered by accident during restoration work on the solar court. The king represents Atum, wearing the double crown of Upper and Lower Egypt.

CHAPTER THREE

HERESY AT AMARNA

WHETHER AS SOLE RULER OR AS COREGENT WITH HIS young son, Amenhotep III celebrated two more jubilees, in Years 34 and 37 of his reign. He died soon after the third and his son took over the throne (or continued as sole ruler). The beginning of the reign of Amenhotep IV, which may have been a sole rule or have overlapped with the later reign of his father, has fascinated both scholars and laypeople. More has been written on this period in Egyptian history than any other, and scholars have been known to come to blows, or at least to major episodes of impoliteness, over their conflicting opinions.

From the outset of his rule, Amenhotep IV is linked with his own great wife, Nefertiti, whose beautiful limestone portrait bust ranks beside the mask of Tutankhamun as one of the most recognizable images from ancient Egypt. Some believe that Nefertiti was a member of Tiye's family, but there is no good evidence for or against this. Like Tiye before her, Nefertiti played an important ritual role in her husband's court.

In the early years of his reign, Amenhotep IV undertook an ambitious building program at Karnak. In order to expedite the rapid building of his temples, his architects employed small blocks that could be carried by a single workman. Although they were in

OPPOSITE: **Head of a Queen** ABOVE: **Head of Amenhotep IV/Akhenaten** This sandstone head of a colossal statue was found at Karnak. The king is shown here as the god Shu, god of the air and son of the creator god Atum.

the main precinct, these temples were, however, not to Amun, but to the sun disk as the Aten. Proponents of the long coregency suggest that the Aten was, in this case, the living senior king, Amenhotep III. Nefertiti, who is given the epithet Neferneferuaten ('Beautiful is the Beauty of the Aten'), features prominently in these monuments; in one of them, she is the sole actor, without her husband beside her, and takes on many of the roles of the pharaoh. One of Akhenaten's primary ritual roles was as the god Shu, son of the creator god Atum; Nefertiti was the incarnation of Tefnut, twin sister and wife of Shu. It has been suggested that Akhenaten and Nefertiti played their roles as Shu and Tefnut in rituals where the living and deified Amenhotep III played the role of Atum.

The art of the new monarch represented a dramatic departure from the idealized images that had been the norm throughout Egyptian history. Changes had begun to creep into the royal styles of his father and grandfather, but the representations of Amenhotep IV and his family were a quantum leap into uncharted territory. The king is shown with an extremely long, narrow face, large chin, narrow shoulders, wide hips, and a sagging belly—a caricature of what was likely his actual appearance. Nefertiti is given the same distorted body shape, as are other members of the court. Volumes have been written about the meaning of these images: The two most current theories, which are not mutually exclusive, are that the king suffered from a genetic disorder called Marfan's syndrome, and that the radical modifications in his art were linked to major changes in royal and religious dogma.

A new theory supporting the long coregency, put forth by a scholar named W. Raymond Johnson, who is now the director of Chicago House in Luxor, has made correlations between the artistic styles under Amenhotep III and Amenhotep IV, arguing that similar modifications occurred at corresponding times. Amenhotep IV/ Akhenaten began his reign using a traditional style, where he is shown with his father's features (a tradition that can be seen in the art of Thutmosis III, who is shown with Hatshepsut's face), but soon moved to the exaggerated style that is the hallmark of his reign. There are many similarities between the late style of Amenhotep III and the exaggerated style of

OPPOSITE: **Stela of Akhenaten** Amarna art showed, for the first time, intimate portraits of the royal family. Here, Akhenaten and Nefertiti bask in the rays of the sun disk with three of their daughters.

his son: the two styles can be explained both as based on individualism and an enhanced naturalism and as theological constructs designed to communicate important religious symbolism to the viewer.

Another series of dramatic transformations took place between Years five and seven, which according to some scholars may mark the beginning of Amenhotep IV's sole rule. The cult of the Aten became ever more important, the sun disk extending arms, rather than rays, to an offering table or towards the royal family. Whether or not the old king was still alive, the Aten was strongly identified with Amenhotep III, thus Amenhotep IV had a very real personal relationship with this deity. At this point, Amenhotep IV changed his name to Akhenaten, which means 'The Transfigured Spirit of the Aten.' The king's supreme god was converted into the sole creator god from whom everything issued. This is expressed in a beautiful hymn inscribed in several of the tombs of this period:

Splendid you rise, O living Aten,
eternal lord!
You are radiant, beauteous, mighty,
Your love is great, immense.
Your rays light up all faces,
Your light here gives life to hearts,
When you fill the Two Lands with
your love.

August god who fashioned himself,
Who made every land, created
what is in it,
All peoples, herds, and flocks,
All trees that grow from soil;
They live when you dawn for them,
You are mother and father of all
that you made.

(Translation by Miram Lichtheim)

As part of his religious revolution, Akhenaten decided to leave Thebes and move to a virgin site that would be dedicated to his new cult, possibly because of a struggle with the priests of Amun. The new city was located in Middle Egypt, and called Akhetaten, 'Horizon of the Aten.' It was laid out parallel to the river, its boundaries marked by stelae carved into the cliffs ringing the site. The king himself took responsibility for its cosmologically significant master plan. In the center of his city, the king built a 'formal reception palace,' where he could meet officials and foreign dignitaries. The palaces in which he and his family lived were to the north, and a road led from the royal dwelling to the reception

palace. Each day, Akhenaten and Nefertiti processed in their chariots from one end of the city to the other, mirroring the journey of the sun across the sky.

In this, as in many other aspects of their lives that have come to us through art and texts, Akhenaten and Nefertiti were seen, or at least saw themselves, as deities in their own right. It was only through them that the Aten could be worshiped: they were both priests and gods. Nefertiti bore six daughters to her husband, and these princesses were an important part of the divine family. In another radical departure from traditional Egyptian art, the girls are shown climbing on their father's lap, bathing in the rays of the sun that shine down upon the idyllic intimacies of the royal family.

Art at Amarna was less exaggerated than the early Theban art of Akhenaten's reign. Naturalism and realism were the hallmarks of the period, although some of the earlier physical oddities, such as wide hips, sagging bellies, and long necks continue to grace the images of the royal family. Some of the works of art that have survived from this period rank among the greatest masterpieces of Egyptian art.

One day in the winter of 1912, a German archaeologist named Ludwig Borchardt was excavating at Tell al-Amarna when he found a beautiful bust of Nerfertiti in the workshop of a sculptor named Thutmosis. There are many stories about this painted limestone head. One says that the German mission covered the head with mud to disguise its beauty, so that during the division of antiquities at the Egyptian Museum in Cairo the curator did not notice its remarkable features. Therefore, the bust was allowed to go to the Berlin Museum. However, Dietrich Wildung, current director of the Berlin Museum, disclaims this story and even has a sign posted near the head stating that it left Egypt legally. Plans were made to return it to Egypt just before World War II, but

ABOVE: **Head of a princess** This young princess, one of six daughters of Akhenaten and Nefertiti, is shown with an unusually broad and extremely elongated skull.

Hitler asked to see it before it left the country, fell in love with it, and refused to let it out of German hands.

When I visited the Berlin Museum for the first time, I could not stop thinking of the moment when I would see the beautiful head of this queen. When I stood before her, I could not believe that this magnificent head had been made by human hands. I laughed to myself, wondering why New Age people had not claimed that artists from Atlantis had made it. This bust of Nefertiti has become synonymous with beauty. The poise of the head on its long neck balanced by the backwards sweep of her blue headdress (the crown of the goddess Tefnut), the fine classic features and the high cheekbones, these have a cool timeless perfection, which is witness to the return of a more traditional style. One of my dreams is one day to visit Nefertiti in the Egyptian Museum. She has been away from her homeland for a long time.

Queen Tiye came with her son to Amarna, and maintained her position within the court. (If, in fact, her husband was still alive, he migiht have come with her, as is suggested by one stele, found in a private home, that depicts the king and queen side by side.) She is depicted in some of the private tombs at Amarna accompanying her son on state occasions or going with him into the temple of the Aten. On the death of Amenhotep III (whether at the outset of his son's reign or partway through), the Mitanni king wrote to Queen Tiye, who had outlived her husband, anxious that the good relations enjoyed during her husband's lifetime should continue during her son's reign. These letters, written expressly to her, are evidence of her continued influence at court and her knowledge of foreign affairs.

Tiye must have died in about the fourteenth year of her son's reign. A plaited lock of her hair was found in the tomb of Tutankhamun, placed in a miniature coffin inscribed with her name. Fragments of a sarcophagus found in Akhenaten's tomb at Amarna suggest that she was originally buried here, and later moved. A mummy found reburied in the tomb of Amenhotep II has been tentatively identified as hers on the basis of comparison of its hair to the hair found in Tutankhamun's tomb and the likeness of its face and skull to that of the 'boy king.'

OPPOSITE: **Canopic jar** The inscriptions on this canopic jar from Tomb 55 have been erased, and the identity of the queen for whom it was carved has therefore been the subject of a great deal of debate. Scholars have, at least for now, settled on Queen Kiya, a secondary wife of Akhenaten's, as the most likely candidate.

In the realm of marriage, Akhenaten followed the traditions of his dynasty: he had at least one wife other than Nefertiti, and probably more. His second wife, given the special title of 'greatly beloved wife of the king,' was named Kiya; she may have been the mother of Tutankhamun (who was born Tutankhaten). Although there is no direct evidence for this theory, Tutankhamun is known to have been a king's son, thus his father must have been either Akhenaten or Amenhotep III. He does not seem to have been a son of Nefertiti, since he does not appear in any of the family portraits (although sons were rarely shown in any case). So if Akhenaten was his father, the most likely candidate for his mother is Kiya. She disappears in about Year 12 of Akhenaten's reign, which is a possible date for Tutankhamun's birth; she may thus either have died in childbirth or been hounded from court (or murdered) by a jealous Nefertiti. On many monuments, Kiya's name was effaced and replaced by the name of Akhenaten and Nefertiti's eldest daughter, Meritaten.

Proponents of a long coregency believe that Amenhotep III died in about the twelfth year of Akhenaten's reign. This year was marked by a big celebration, known as a durbhar, illustrated in some of the private tombs at Amarna, in which tribute was brought to the king from all of his foreign vassals. According to the believers in the coregency, this was to mark the beginning of the junior king's promotion to senior king; according to believers in a short coregency or the consecutive rules of Amenhotep III and his son, this was simply a normal ceremony of tribute that might have occurred at regular intervals.

At about the same time, Nefertiti either disappears from the historical record or became her husband's coregent as Neferneferuaten Ankh(et)kheperurua. Another theory holds that Nefertiti was banished when Queen Tiye arrived at Amarna to live and Meritaten took over the role of principal queen. A second daughter-queen, Meketaten, was buried within her father's rock-cut tomb in the Amarna cliffs; the wall decoration indicates that she died in childbirth.

Also dating to this point in Akhenaten's reign was a campaign to excise the name of gods other than the Aten, especially Amun, from the monuments of Egypt. This was done with violence: hieroglyphs were brutally hacked from the walls of temples and tombs. This was probably carried out, at least in part, by illiterate iconoclasts, presumably following the orders of their king. A stele dating from the reign of Tutankhamun states that the king inherited a country

Amarna princesses This lively and colorful painting was found at Amarna. This facsimile by Nina Davies shows two of the daughters of Akhenaten and Nefertiti at the feet of the queen; the entire scene depicted all six princesses.

in shambles, its temples neglected and its gods abandoned. If there was, in fact, a long coregency, the temples might have stayed open at least until the end of Amenhotep III's reign; what happened after Year 12 of Akhenaten's rule is open to interpretation and reinterpretation in any case. We know for certain that the cult of the Aten replaced the cult of Amun as the primary state cult, but people certainly continued to worship some traditional gods, even at Amarna. What-ever the details, there is no doubt that Akhenaten, either on his own or with his father, carried out a religious revolution the like of which had never been seen before in Egypt. His reign represents a significant departure from religious, artistic, and political norms.

Akhenaten did not, however, abandon the rest of the country and retire exclusively to Akhetaten. When he laid out his city, he also commanded that a series of boundary stelae be carved in the cliffs surrounding the site. Among other things, these state that he were to die outside of his home city, his body should be brought back and buried in the tomb that was being prepared for him in the eastern cliffs. There is evidence that, as Amenhotep IV, he carried out building projects in Nubia, and there were temples to the Aten in Memphis and Heliopolis, and possibly elsewhere as well. Although the religious capital of the country was moved from Thebes to Amarna, Memphis may well have continued as a key center of administration. The tomb of one of his viziers, a man possibly of foreign lineage named Aperel, was found recently at Saqqara; this man first served under Amenhotep III, and also held the title of high priest of the Aten. The tomb of another high priest of Aten, Meryneith, was discovered here in 2001 by a Dutch expedition. Another vizier from the early part of his reign, Ramose, prepared his tomb at Thebes. In fact, the number of officials that planned to be buried in the necropolis at Amarna is relatively low, as indicated by the number of decorated tombs carved into the cliffs. Given the size of the population of Akhetaten, it is also quite puzzling that a large cemetery has not been found there; this may indicate that the inhabitants preferred to be buried in their home towns, or may simply be because the principal cemetery has not yet been found.

An important archive of foreign correspondence with Egypt's vassals and allies was stumbled upon accidentally in 1887 by a peasant woman who was collecting ancient mud brick to use as fertilizer. These letters, written on clay tablets in the lingua franca of the day, Akkadian, include missives to Amenhotep III, Akhenaten, Tiye, and Nefertiti (and possibly also to Tutankhamun and Ay); several of them have been referred to above. They paint the picture of a world of luxury, where gold was as plentiful as dust, but also, in the letters to Akhenaten, of an inward-focused regime that had lost interest in its foreign policy. A series of letters from one vassal ruler begs for help from Egypt against marauding tribesmen, but it is clear that no aid was

OPPOSITE: **Meryneith and his wife** A number of Akhenaten's top officials chose to be buried at Saqqara, including this high priest of the Aten, Meryneith, seen here with his wife. Their tomb was discovered relatively recently, proving that there are still many treasures hidden beneath the sands of Egypt.

forthcoming from the Amarna court. A major shift of influence in the Near East began during Akhenaten's reign, perhaps even due to his neglect of the empire: Egypt's old enemy and erstwhile ally, the Mitanni, were threatened by their old foes, the Hittites, who were rapidly becoming the dominant power in Syria-Palestine.

Akhenaten died in the seventeenth year of his reign. He may have been succeeded by a shadowy king named Smenkhkare, to whom very few monuments can be attributed. In 1907, an American named Theodore Davis, whom we shall meet again later, sponsored excavations in the Valley of the Kings that uncovered an enigmatic burial known as Tomb 55. The tomb had been robbed, and the furnishings inside badly damaged, but it still contained a mix of materials bearing the names of Queen Tiye, Akhenaten himself, Amenhotep III, Queen Kiya, and Tutankhamun.

Scholars who have studied this tomb believe that Queen Tiye, who, as we have seen, was buried first in the tomb of her son at Amarna, was moved here, along with a beautiful wooden canopy and some of her funerary equipment. She was later moved again, perhaps to the tomb of Amenhotep II, where a mummy nicknamed the Elder Woman, and believed to be Tiye, still lies. In a gilded wooden coffin, built originally for Akhenaten's greatly beloved wife Kiya and then altered to hold the body of a king lay the mummy of a young man, aged approximately twenty-five. The face of this coffin had been ripped away, and the names chiseled out, as if to destroy the identity of the man who lay inside. It was long believed that this body was Smenkhkare. Conspiracy theories abounded, and continue to circulate. If this was indeed Smenkhkare, was he assassinated by Nefertiti? Or was he killed by an older man named Ay, eventual successor to Tutankhamun and possibly a relative of Nefertiti's? Perhaps Nefertiti, or Ay, or the two together, did not like that Smenkhkare was king and conspired with the priests of Amun, who must certainly have been against the Amarna revolution, to kill him and put the malleable child, Tutankhaten, on the throne.

OPPOSITE: **Coffin from Tomb 55** The question of who was buried in Tomb 55 has long plagued scholars. The bones of a man, aged about twenty-five to thirty at death, were found in the tomb, within this royal coffin. Whoever he was, his memory had been desecrated—his cartouches removed and his face hacked away. Scholars now believe that this may have been Akhenaten himself.

It is now believed that the body in Tomb 55 is most likely Akhenaten himself, who, especially if he ruled with his father for a number of years, might well have been only in his late twenties or early thirties when he died. His rock-cut tomb at Amarna was never completed, but fragments of a red granite sarcophagus (a material associated with the solar cult) with figures of Nefertiti on all four sides, arms outstretched to embrace the remains of the king, were found inside, next to the sarcophagus of his mother. Both royal bodies, however, were missing. The Tomb 55 mummy is thus a reasonable candidate for the body of the heretic king himself.

But if the body in Tomb 55 is Akhenaten himself, then where is Smenkhkare? Some scholars would now like to identify this king as Nefertiti herself. This king is shown as a male in the company of Meritaten as 'his' queen; however, his throne name was virtually identical to that of Akhenaten's coregent, now convincingly identified as Nefertiti. Whether this king was Nefertiti herself or an otherwise unattested son of Akhenaten's (or Amenhotep III's), he or she died only two years after ascending the throne, and left Egypt in the hands of a young boy named Tutankhaten.

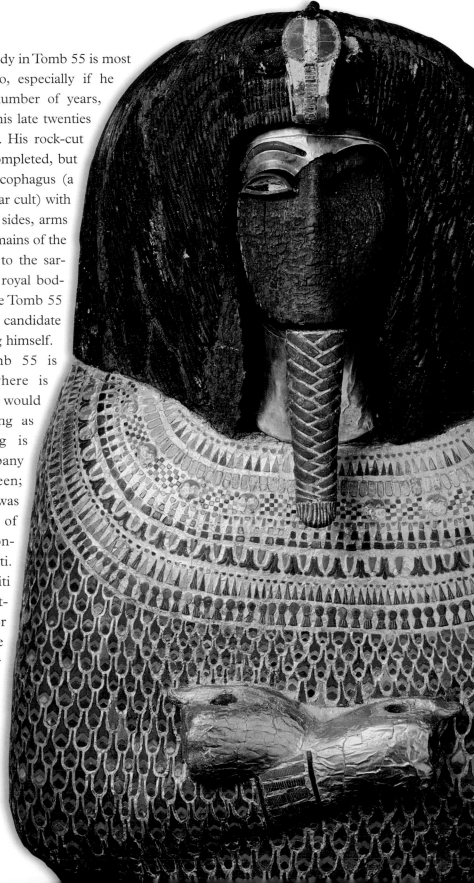

CHAPTER FOUR

THE LIFE OF TUTANKHAMUN

TUTANKHAMUN WAS BORN IN ABOUT YEAR 11 OF THE REIGN OF Akhenaten. He most likely came into the world at Amarna, and was named Tutankhaten, 'living image of the Aten.' It is possible that he was the son of Amenhotep III and Queen Tiye, although this only works if a long coregency between Amenhotep III and Akhenaten is assumed. Otherwise, Tutankhaten would have been over the age of seventeen when he took the throne of Egypt. In fact, most scholars believe that Tutankhaten was the son of Akhenaten and Kiya, but the balance of opinion may yet change.

The young prince would have grown up in the royal palace at Amarna, under the care of royal nurses. The tomb of his wet nurse, a woman named Maya, has recently been discovered at Saqqara, near Memphis. This was a beautifully decorated tomb; clearly Maya held high status in the boy-king's court. Based on the various palatial remains found at Amarna, as well as the palace at Malqata, the young prince's home probably contained a central ornamental pool surrounded by rectangular units, an open sun court with an altar, a stable for cattle (complete with mangers), and a formal garden with exquisite wall paintings of nature, for example of birds in papyrus marshes. In the formal reception palace at Amarna, one painted floor, found intact, depicts a rectangular pool alive with fish and water plants surrounded by gamboling calves and ducks flying out of clumps of reeds and papyrus. This type of naturalistic decoration, which may also have had symbolic function, is likely to have been prominent in Tutankhaten's palace as well.

OPPOSITE: **Golden fan base of Tutankhamun**

Marsh scene The palaces of the New Kingdom were painted with lively scenes covering a wide range of topics. This fragment from a decorated floor shows a bird in the papyrus marshes in the naturalistic Amarna style.

Many of the objects in Tutankhamun's tomb bear witness to his marriage to Ankhsenpaaten, fourth of Nefertiti and Akhenaten's six daughters. Perhaps, after the death of his own mother, the young Tutankhaten was taken to live with his bride-to-be's mother. The two children must have grown up together, and perhaps playing together in the palace gardens. The royal children would have had lessons from teachers and scribes, who would have given them instruction in wisdom and knowledge about the new religion of the Aten. It is likely that Akhenaten wanted his children to continue with the worship of Aten, not to go back to the old religion dedicated to Amun. It also seems likely, especially if Nefertiti and Smenkhkare were one and the same person, that the great queen arranged the marriage between her daughter and the new king. Following the marriage would have come a celebration for the whole country, where people could dance, sing, feast, and tell stories. Perhaps some of the protective deities, particularly the goddess Hathor, were invoked to ensure a happy outcome for the bride and groom.

Tutankhaten and Ankhsenpaaten would probably have been married to one another at a very young age, almost certainly for reasons of state, but perhaps they also loved one another. To judge from their portrayal in the art that fills the golden king's tomb, this was certainly the case. We can feel the love between them as we see the queen standing in front of her husband giving him flowers and accompanying him while he was hunting. Of course, these scenes have religious significance—in addition to her role as wife and queen, Ankhsenpaaten plays the roles of various goddesses, and the actions she is depicted performing help to insure the rebirth of the king and the proper order of the universe. But I prefer to believe that they were also in love.

It is tempting to imagine the child-bride sitting in her room thinking about her new husband. Perhaps she sent him a beautiful flower, or wrote him letters of love. She would have addressed him as brother and talked to him openly. In love poetry written during the New Kingdom, a young girl admits that she is smitten: "My brother torments my heart with his voice. He makes sickness take hold of me." She complains that she cannot control her heart: "My heart flutters hastily, when I think of my love of you; it lets me not act sensibly, it leaps [from] its place . . . Be steady when you think of him, my heart, do not flutter!"

The young man is suffering likewise: "Seven days since I saw my sister, and sickness invaded me . . . . When the physicians come to me, my heart rejects their remedies . . . . My sister is better than all prescriptions . . . the sight of her makes me well!" (Translations by Miriam Lichtheim)

Tutankhaten was only eight or nine years old when he came to the throne. In his tomb were many items prepared for his use as a child-king—miniature emblems of office, such as a small crook and flail, small bows, quivers, and staffs; and furniture designed for a child. A number of these were inscribed with his birth name, demonstrating that he was crowned as Tutankhaten.

FOLLOWING PAGES: **Golden throne** A number of elaborate chairs were found in the tomb of Tutankhamun. This is one of the most elaborate of these, as it is covered with gold leaf and inlaid with semi-precious stones. The central scene depicts the young king seated on a throne while his queen anoints him with oil.

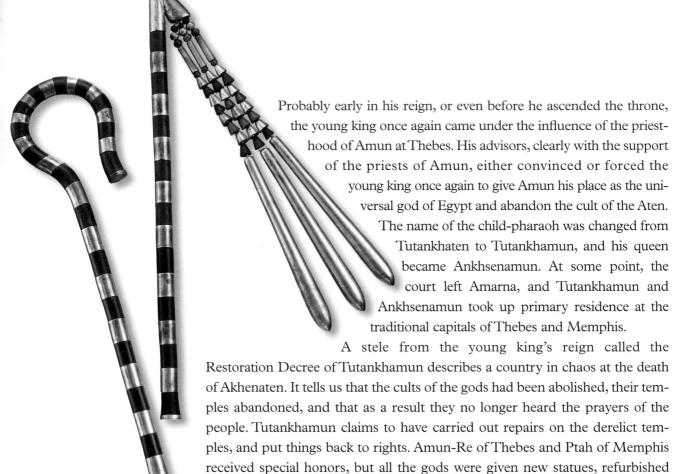

Probably early in his reign, or even before he ascended the throne, the young king once again came under the influence of the priesthood of Amun at Thebes. His advisors, clearly with the support of the priests of Amun, either convinced or forced the young king once again to give Amun his place as the universal god of Egypt and abandon the cult of the Aten. The name of the child-pharaoh was changed from Tutankhaten to Tutankhamun, and his queen became Ankhsenamun. At some point, the court left Amarna, and Tutankhamun and Ankhsenamun took up primary residence at the traditional capitals of Thebes and Memphis.

A stele from the young king's reign called the Restoration Decree of Tutankhamun describes a country in chaos at the death of Akhenaten. It tells us that the cults of the gods had been abolished, their temples abandoned, and that as a result they no longer heard the prayers of the people. Tutankhamun claims to have carried out repairs on the derelict temples, and put things back to rights. Amun-Re of Thebes and Ptah of Memphis received special honors, but all the gods were given new statues, refurbished temples, and refilled coffers.

We know that Tutankhamun must have participated in the many important religious festivals that required the divine presence of the king. These included the feast of Opet at Karnak and Luxor, the celebration of which was recorded in detail on the walls of the Luxor temple, and the Harvest Festival of Min. At the major temples, Tutankhamun and his queen would have had a small ceremonial palace, complete with a reception area, throne room, and private chambers, including bathrooms for royal use.

The 'golden king' would have used his palace at Thebes for important religious festivals, and various rest-houses scattered around the country for hunting trips up and down the country. He would have learned how to ride horses and drive the chariots that were buried with him in his tomb. When he become stronger, perhaps at the age of ten, he would have begun his training in military skills in

ABOVE: Crook and flail Tutankhamun himself may have held this pair of royal implements at ceremonies of state. On the base of these items, made of blue glass and metal, is the cartouche of the king.

the desert of Memphis to the north. In the 1920s, a royal rest house built during the reign of Tutankhamun was discovered at Giza, just south of Khafre's Valley Temple. Some scholars believe that Tutanhamun, like many of the kings of the Eighteenth Dynasty, was trained at Memphis. This seems to have been in use from the time of Tutankhamun until at least the Ramesside Period. In addition to its use as a hunting lodge, it would have been used during religious observances at the nearby Sphinx, worshipped as the sun god Horemakhet. Unfortunately, excavators eager to reach earlier levels below removed this villa without proper records.

Since we have no physical remains, we can only imagine the principal residence of Tutankhamun and his queen. It, like the palace of Malkata and the palaces at Amarna, would have been built of mud brick and beautifully painted. It would have consisted of many large rooms and columned halls surrounded by smaller suites of rooms. The largest of these would have been for the king and would have contained a series of larger halls leading to a throne room. These would have been decorated with lively scenes of birds and natural motifs. There would have been gardens and pools, all designed to soothe and delight the royal eyes and ears.

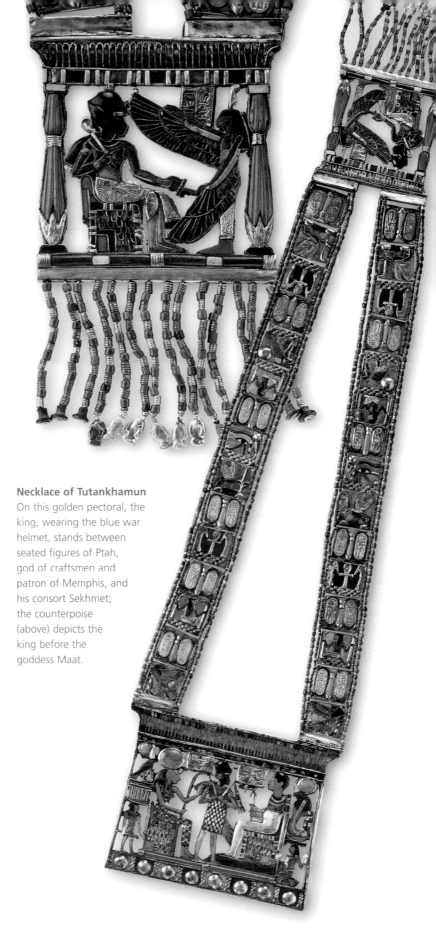

Necklace of Tutankhamun
On this golden pectoral, the king, wearing the blue war helmet, stands between seated figures of Ptah, god of craftsmen and patron of Memphis, and his consort Sekhmet; the counterpoise (above) depicts the king before the goddess Maat.

King Tutankhamun, like all New Kingdom pharaohs, had five names. He had a Horus name, which associated him with the great sky god who took the form of a falcon; this was 'Strong Bull, fitting of created forms.' His Two Ladies name, which afforded him protection from the tutelary goddesses of Upper and Lower Egypt, and his golden Horus name each come in a number of variations. The two names by which we know him best were his throne name, Nebkheperure, and his birth name (or in this case, modified birth name), Tutankhamun Heqa Iunushema (Living image of Amun, ruler of Southern Heliopolis). These last two names are the ones found written on most of his monuments. The epithet attached to his birth name is very interesting, as it links Thebes ('Southern Heliopolis') with the northern cult center of the sun god.

By the reign of Tutankhamun the situation in the Near East had changed drastically since the golden days of the Egyptian empire. The Restoration text claims that "if an army [was] sent to Djahy (in western Asia), to broaden the boundaries of Egypt, no success of theirs came to pass . . . ." The rise of the Hittites had shattered the delicate peace that had been maintained for two generations, and some of Egypt's vassal states had been lost. A campaign undertaken either late in the reign of Akhenaten or during the reign of his immediate successor to Syria to retake the key city of Qadesh apparently ended in defeat. A stalemate had been reached, which remained until Tutankhamun's ninth year of reign, when the Egyptian army again attacked Qadesh, most likely under the commander of the army, Horemheb. This high official, who held many important titles under Tutankhamun and seems to have outranked even the viziers, built a spectacular tomb for himself in the Memphite necropolis, the cemetery where a number of the notables of Tutankhamun's reign were buried. But again, the army was unsuccessful, and the Hittites took advantage of the situation and attacked the Mitanni, defeating them decisively and wiping both their empire and their kingdom from the map.

OPPOSITE: **Chest in the shape of a cartouche** Many chests and boxes were found in the tomb. This example is shaped like a cartouche, symbol of the circuit of the sun. On top is the name of the king: Tutankhamun, ruler of Southern Helio-polis—the beautifully detailed hieroglyphs are carefully inlaid with ebony and ivory.

THE DEATH OF THE GOLDEN KING

Tutankhamun died in January of 1327, when he was only about eighteen years old. Egyptologists have estimated the season of his death through analysis of the fruits and the flowers found in his tomb. Perhaps the queen herself laid a bouquet of flowers on her husband's coffin as a greeting and a goodbye to her lover, king, and husband, who left her alone and went to the other world without her companionship. Much has been written about the mysterious death of the young king; it has even been suggested by a number of people that he was murdered. However, there is no real evidence for this, and many people died young in ancient times. In addition, it is possible that Tutankhamun, like Akhenaten, suffered from a genetic disorder that could have shortened his lifespan.

OPPOSITE: **North wall of tomb of Tutankhamun**
One of the first tasks of any new king was the burial of his predecessor. By making sure that the burial rites were carried out properly, the monarch, in this case Ay, would secure his place in the succession.

Tutankhamun and Ankhsenamun left no children behind them. We know that the queen became pregnant at least twice, but her children were stillborn. One was a girl who died at the age of about seven months gestation. The other, whose gender is uncertain, seems to have had a congenital deformity and died at birth. These two fetuses were buried in their father's tomb—carefully mummified and placed in miniature nests of coffins. Perhaps the king and queen were still too young to have children, or perhaps they were too closely related genetically to produce viable offspring. We know that at least one, if not two, of Ankhsenamun's sisters had already died in childbirth; we think that, although her children died, the queen herself survived.

The country would have fallen in disorder at the sudden death of Tutankhamun, who left the land with no heir. At the moment of his death, it is possible that Egypt was engaged in battle with the Hittites, in which case it is likely that Horemheb, who might otherwise have been expected to take the throne, was in the north leading the troops. Another high official, Ay, supervised the king's trip to the afterlife instead.

Ay bore the titles of Commander of Chariotry and Fanbearer at the

King's Right Hand. In addition, he was a God's Father, and it has been suggested, on the basis of both his name and his titles, that he was a member of either Tiye's family, Nefertiti's family, or, if Tiye and Nefertiti were related, both. In any event, by taking charge of the burial of the previous king, Ay assured his place on the throne of the Two Lands. According to Egyptian mythology, Horus took charge of the burial of his father, Osiris, and by doing so, secured his right to the throne of Egypt. Each crown prince, each heir, was responsible for burying his father, and thereby presented himself to the country as the next Horus. By burying Tutankhamun, Ay proclaimed himself the next king.

If Tutankhamun planned a great tomb for himself in the Valley of the Kings, he did not have a chance to finish it. He was buried instead in a small tomb, of the sort carved out of the rock for private people privileged enough to be buried in the valley but not of the stature of a king. This tomb, which may have even been planned originally for Ay himself, was finished and decorated within the seventy days that it took to prepare the royal mummy.

Work on the tomb would probably have been directed by Maya, treasurer of Tutankhamun and the overseer of construction in the necropolis. Ay, Maya, another military officer named Nakhtmin, and the other high officials of the king would each have had a role to play in the funeral, the tomb construction and decoration, and in preparing gifts for the king to take with him to the afterlife. We can imagine Ay announcing the death of the king, and the country going into mourning. All the officials and viziers might have stopped working, turning their attention instead to their duties to the deceased pharaoh.

The period between death and burial was seventy days. The priests would have moved Tutankhamun's body to the mummification tent, the *per-nefer* ('good house'), where the process of embalming would have been carried out. First, the internal organs were removed through an incision in the left side. The lungs, liver, stomach, and intestines were removed and dried, wrapped, and placed in four golden canopic coffinettes, which were in turn placed inside an alabaster container with

OPPOSITE: **Shabti of Tutankhamun** Many shabti figures were found in the tomb of the golden king. In this beautiful wooden statuette, the king wears the so-called Nubian wig. FOLLOWING PAGES: **Canopic chest of Tutankhamun** During the process of mummification, the lungs, liver, stomach, and intestines of the young king were removed, treated, wrapped separately, and placed in inlaid golden coffinnettes, which were then stored in the compartments of this calcite chest. The sides are inscribed with protective spells, and the stoppers represent the king himself.

four sections, topped with four beautifully carved heads of the king. The heart, thought to be the seat of intelligence, was left in place. The brain, which decays and becomes soft, was extracted through a hole pierced through the nasal cavity.

The embalming process continued until the mummy was ready to go into the tomb. When the body had been stripped of all moisture, the wrapping process began. A beaded cap decorated with royal cobras covered his head; protective necklaces and pectorals were hung around his neck and placed on his chest; bracelets were clasped around his wrists and forearms; heavy rings weighed down his fingers, their nails covered by golden fingerstalls; and several daggers, one of iron, were placed at his waist and groin. By the end of this process, the mummy of Tutankhamun was adorned and protected by 143 amulets and jewels, most of them of gold.

At the end of seventy days, the body, now transformed into an image of the god Osiris that would last for eternity, was taken on its final journey to the tomb. Since Tutankhamun did not have a son, the chief mortuary priest, together with Ay, conducted a special ceremony known as the Opening of the Mouth in front of the tomb. This ritual insured that the mummy of the king was vivified so that it would be able to receive offerings. During the rites, two women enacted the roles of Isis and Nephthys, sisters and wives of Osiris, mourning for their dead love. In many cases these women were from the royal palace, but there were professional mourners who also impersonated the two goddesses for a fee. The mummy was placed upright on a heap of sand and the mouth, eyes, and nose were touched with various implements in order to restore the senses and enable the ba (part of the soul) to return to the body. Then a complicated offering and ritual ensured that, through the presentation of food, drink, incense and many other things, the ka of the king would be strengthened and could live forever.

After the Opening of the Mouth, the body was lowered down the shaft to the Burial Chamber and all the other things that had accompanied the funeral procession were put in place. In Tutankhamun's case, many of the objects placed in the tomb had originally been prepared for other royal burials, and were adapted for his use. The tomb was then closed and stamped with the seals of the necropolis guardians, expected to remain inviolate for eternity.

Dagger and Sheath

The mummy of Tutankhamun was accompanied by two daggers, one at his waist and the other placed alongside his thigh. The blade of the example shown here is of solid gold ornamented with a palmette design. The handle is decorated with geometric patterns and floral motifs. The gold sheath is beautifully decorated with hunting scenes.

65

CHAPTER FIVE

THE AFTERMATH

WE MIGHT IMAGINE THE YOUNG QUEEN OF TUTANKHAMUN sitting alone in the palace, thinking that she would now be forced to marry Ay, already an old man. She might have wept for the loss of her lover and king, remembering the first days of their love at Amarna, when they ran and played together. Maybe Ankhsenamun smiled to herself as she thought of the moment when Tutankhamun tried to kiss her for the first time. But she was a queen, and a servant of Egypt, and at some point during this time of mourning and healing from her great loss, she realized, perhaps with the help of one of her close friends and advisors, that she must think first of Egypt. So the young Queen chose one of her most trusted soldiers and asked him to deliver a letter to the Hittite king, Suppiluliumas. Perhaps she even warned him to be wary of two people in particular, Ay and General Horemheb, although it is possible that Ay was also involved in the plot. A copy of this letter was found in the Hittite archives discovered at their capital in Anatolia. It reads, "My husband has died and I have no son. They say that you have many sons. You might give me one of your sons and he might become my husband. I would not want to take one of my servants. I am loath to make him my husband." The queen offers peace between Hatti (the land of the Hittites) and Egypt, saying that the two empires could become one country.

Suppiluliumas must have been astounded, knowing that such a thing had never happened before. Egyptian kings married foreign princesses, but it was unheard of for an Egyptian princess, let alone a queen, to marry a foreign

OPPOSITE: **Gilded wooden shield of Tutankhamun**

prince. So he sent an envoy to check this extraordinary request. The envoy returned with a second letter: "I have not written to any other country, I have written only to you . . . . He will be my husband and king in the country of Egypt." Reassured, the king dispatched one of his sons on the long journey south. But the prince never reached Egypt; he died en route, a victim most likely either of assassination or of plague.

It was once thought that these letters were from Nefertiti, written after the death of Akhenaten. However, scholarly opinion is now leaning toward Ankh-senamun as the author of these pleas for help. We do not have any records to tell us what exactly happened after Ankhesenamun sent her letters to the Hittite king. Perhaps Ay told the commander of the army, Horemheb, what the young queen had done, or perhaps Ay and Horemheb were themselves involved in a struggle for the throne. Perhaps the two men decided together to stop the Hittite prince, because it would have brought shame on the nation for an Egyptian queen to marry a foreigner—such a thing would have reversed the proper order of things. Perhaps it was Ay, or his successor, Horemheb, who had the Hittite prince killed; and perhaps Akhsenamun was forced, after all, to marry the aged Ay. In fact, we do not have any clues to her eventual fate. Her name is not mentioned in Ay's tomb, which is located in the Valley of the Kings, where we see only the name of his principal wife, Tiye.

Whatever the eventual fate of Ankhsenamun, we know that Ay ruled for only three years. He died without an heir, and was buried in the Valley of the Kings, in a tomb that is a close copy of Tutankhamun's. The throne passed to the Commander of the Army, Horemheb. Under the long rule (at least fifty-nine years) of this king, the Amarna period began to be wiped from the memory of the Egyptians. Since he was of non-royal blood, Horemheb claims to have been chosen by Horus of Hutsenu to rule Egypt. The return to orthodoxy had already begun, even before Tutankhamun

OPPOSITE: **Statue of the god Amun** This beautiful greywacke statue of the god Amun was found in the courtyard of the cachette at Karnak. The upper part of the crown, which would have depicted the high feathers that characterize this god, was worked separately and has now been lost. **FOLLOWING PAGES: Funerary mask of Tutankhamun** This, one of the most famous artifacts in the world, was found covering the head of the mummy of Tutankhamun. The serene face of the young king gazes at us across more than thirty centuries, attesting to the skill of the ancient artisans and the wealth of the royal house.

ascended the throne, and great progress in restoring the traditional cults had already been made. It was left to Horemheb to complete the country's return to its ancient traditions: Among other acts, he destroyed the Aten temples at Karnak and branded Akhenaten 'that enemy of Akhetaten.' He tried, in fact, to erase all evidence of Akhenaten and his immediate successors from the pages of history. But he could not rid the land of all traces of the Amarna episode. Its echoes lingered on in the art of the later New Kingdom, in many aspects of religion, and even in the written word.

However, Horemheb's bid to wipe the memory of the heretic king and his offspring from Egyptian history worked, and at least by the reign of Ramesses VI the boy-king had been forgotten. The entrance to his tomb was no longer visible, and the workers who carved the tomb of Ramesses VI built their huts right on top of it, completely obscuring it from view and keeping it safe for the next three millennia. By effectively wiping the name of Tutankhamun from the annals of the pharaohs, Horemheb actually succeeded in insuring that the name of the golden king would resound through the corridors of time.

CHAPTER SIX

ROBBERS IN THE VALLEY OF THE KINGS

THE VALLEY OF THE KINGS IS ONE OF THE MOST ROMANTIC SITES in the world. It is situated on the west bank of the Nile, across the river from modern-day Luxor. 'Valley' is actually a misnomer; in reality, it is a complex of wadis, dry streambeds that cut into the cliffs that line the low desert bordering the river.

The first king whom we are sure was buried in the valley is Thutmosis I; his mortuary temple was constructed in the low desert, close to the flood plain. Thus the tomb and its temple were separated, and the tomb hidden in what turned out to be a vain attempt to foil ancient tomb robbers. Believing that he had accomplished his goal of protecting the immortal pharaoh, the royal architect, Ineni, inscribed these words on the wall of his own tomb: "I built the tomb of my majesty, no one seeing, no one hearing."

In many ways, Ineni continued the designs of the ancient past. His plan imitated the style of the royal mortuary complexes of the First Dynasty at Abydos, with the tombs located in one area (far out in the desert) and the mortuary temples in another (close to the edge of the floodplain). Ineni also made reference to the sacred pyramid under which the kings of the Old and Middle Kingdoms were buried in his selection of the tomb site for his king. The Valley of the Kings lies beneath a pyramid, but not one of human creation; rather it is formed by a natural pyramid-shaped hill known as the Qurn. Ineni also learned from the pyramids of the Old and Middle Kingdoms, which had been looted by this time. By secreting the royal tomb in the crevices of the rocky Theban landscape rather than marking its exact location with a huge artificial mountain, he hoped to preserve its contents for eternity.

OPPOSITE: **Coffin from Tomb 55**

Over the span of many centuries sixty-two tombs were hidden in the Valley of the Kings. Most of these tombs belonged to pharaohs, although several were for especially favored courtiers or family members. Queens were for the most part buried in another wadi nearby, now known as the Valley of the Queens. The valley continued in use until the Twenty-first Dynasty, when it was abandoned in favor of burials within temple precincts. Tutankhamun was the seventh pharaoh to be buried in the valley and Ramesses X was the last.

By the time the valley was abandoned, most of the tombs had been robbed of their furnishings. Tomb robbers had breached the security of many of these burials, some soon after the royal bodies had been laid to rest. Tomb robbery was most likely an ancient profession; the great pyramids of the Old Kingdom had been robbed by the Middle Kingdom, and the Middle Kingdom pyramids were emptied by the start of the New Kingdom. The smuggling of Egyptian treasures goes back more than five thousand years.

The desecration of the tombs in the Valley of the Kings began almost immediately. For example, robbers entered the tomb of Tutankhamun twice, most likely soon after it was first sealed. Fortunately, it was saved both times by the necropolis police, although many portable and saleable items were removed. In fact, it has been estimated that about 60 percent of the jewelry from one room in particular was stolen in ancient times. Ay would have been responsible for resealing the tomb; his officials threw the remaining goods back into some sort of order and resealed the tomb, replastering the opening cut by the robbers and stamping it again with the official seal.

Robbery of the royal tombs increased during the Ramesside period. The thieves first focused their attention to the tombs of the nobles and officials, and then extended their activities to the tombs of the kings. The robbers of

The Valley of the Kings The pharaohs of the New Kingdom had their tombs hidden in the rocky crevices of the two wadis that form the Valley of the Kings, hoping to escape the robbers who had plundered the tombs of their ancestors.

this period were supported by many of the people on the west bank of Thebes, including the police, because they gave out many bribes.

Papyri dating from the Ramesside Period (c. 1295–1069) provide us with a fascinating glimpse of one group of antiquities thieves. The picture painted in this archive depicts jealousy and competition developing between the mayor of the east bank of Thebes, a man named Paser, and the mayor of west bank, Pawera, who was responsible for guarding the safety of the royal tombs. According to this text, Paser, the mayor of the east bank, wrote a report to the vizier of Egypt informing him about the involvement of the mayor of the west bank in the robbery of the tombs. The vizier requested that an investigation be started. A committee was appointed, but their report took the side of the mayor of the west bank, stating that they had investigated nine tombs in the royal area and found them in good condition. In addition, they noted that the two queens' tombs they had checked were intact, but that some artifacts from the tombs of the nobles had been scattered about. The committee concluded that Paser, the mayor of the east bank was a liar. Of course, Pawera was very happy because the committee was on his side. We can imagine him collecting his men and crossing to the east bank, laughing, and shouting at Paser as they celebrated their victory in the streets, perhaps even fighting and shouting at one another in front of Paser's house.

The next day, Paser went again to the vizier and made another report. The investigation was reopened. This time the thieves and the people who worked for the mayor of the west bank told the truth. The evidence collected has been preserved in a group of papyri, which list by name a number of the tombs that were robbed, and even count the number of artifacts taken. It is very interesting to read the judgment from the papyri, translated by my colleague Andrea MacDowell. It reads:

> The vizier, the two butlers, the herald of pharaoh, the mayor of East Thebes Paser and the great magistrates of the Kenbet handed over to the high priest of Amun three men found guilty of robbing the tomb of King Sebekemsaf and one man found to have robbed private tombs. They instructed the high priest to capture the thieves who had escaped and to imprison all of these men in the temple of Amun until the pharaoh had decided their punishment.

Years later the fate of the thieves from the time of the vizier Khem was remembered as a warning to those who considered a career in tomb robbery that they might pay with their lives. It would not be surprising if this were a reference to these very men.

After the Twentieth Dynasty came to an end, the Valley of the Kings was no longer used for royal burials. It must have been difficult to police the now abandoned area, and it is likely that the thieves became bolder. The final violation of the royal tombs may have been carried out under the official sanction of the high priests and kings of the Twenty-first Dynasty. We know that these men had the bodies of their royal ancestors gathered up, stripped of some of their remaining valuables, rewrapped, labeled, and hidden away in caches, where they were found in modern times (see below). They may have done this primarily out of piety, but they may also have been motivated by the treasures still hidden with the ancient kings, which they could use to fund their own administrations and equip their own tombs. Whichever is the case, we must thank the kings of the Twenty-first Dynasty, because without their efforts, many of the royal mummies would not have been saved.

Unfortunately, tomb robbery is not a thing of the past; terrible crimes still take place today. The antiquities market has an insatiable appetite for ancient artifacts, so tomb robbers still try to pillage the valley in the dead of the night. We, the protectors of the monuments, work diligently trying to stop them and protect the artifacts and tombs as well as the integrity and spiritual value of the pharaohs, but it is an uphill battle. Until people learn to place more importance on understanding our shared past than in owning bits of it, we will have to continue the struggle.

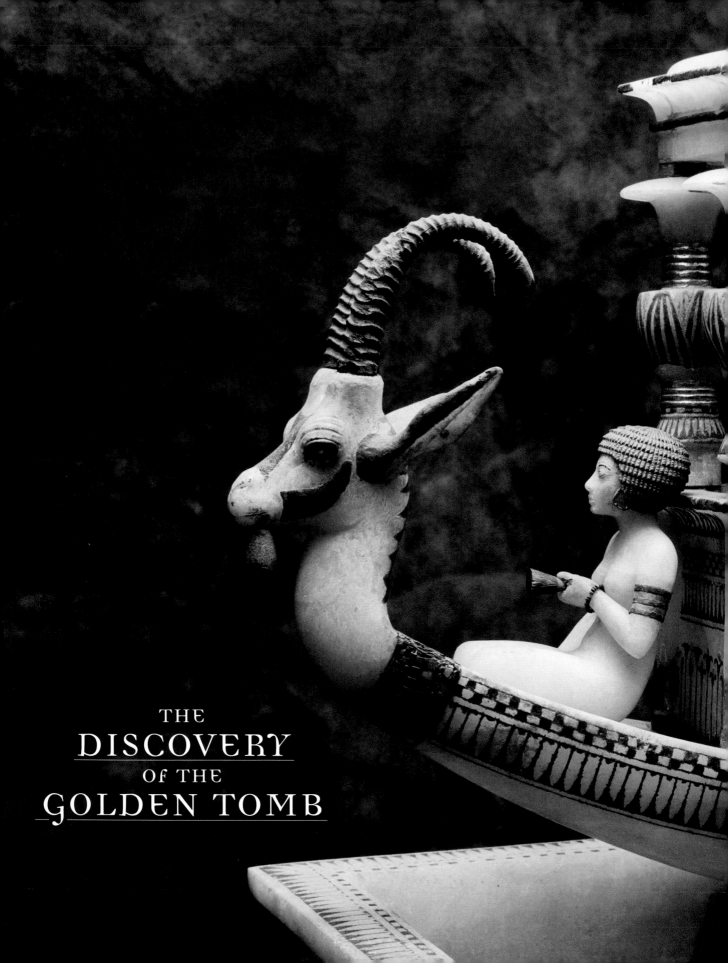

THE
DISCOVERY
OF THE
GOLDEN TOMB

Alabaster bark on a basin

CHAPTER SEVEN

EARLY EXCAVATIONS
IN THE VALLEY OF THE KINGS

BETWEEN ANTIQUITY AND THE NINETEENTH CENTURY, THE Theban area was relatively difficult to reach and visited only by the most intrepid Europeans. In 1708, when a French Jesuit priest named Claude Sicard made his way (escorted, to be sure, by local guides) to the Valley of the Kings, he found ten tombs open. The next western traveler to leave a record of his explorations was an Englishman named Richard Pococke, who in the late 1730s was able to enter nine tombs and noted about nine more. The first intensive explorations were carried out by a team of French scientists in the wake of Napoleon's expedition to Egypt (1799–1801); these men copied a number of the wall reliefs and paintings in the accessible royal tombs, and published them in their monumental *Description de l'Égypte*. Over the course of the next century, a number of scholars and artists visited the valley and made records of what they saw, again including copies of the paintings and reliefs on the walls of the accessible tombs. It is instructive to compare different versions of the same scene made by different artists—an element of artistic interpretation was usually present to a greater or lesser extent.

A number of important tombs were discovered during the nineteenth century. Giovanni Belzoni, an Italian strongman and engineer turned adventurer–archaeologist, came to the valley in 1815 or 1816 in the service of the British Consul-General, Henry Salt. Salt was an avid collector of antiquities, and sent Belzoni to the valley to get the sarcophagus of Ramesses III (c. 1184–1153 B.C.). The mission, which required all of Belzoni's engineering expertise, was successful, and Belzoni stayed on to

OPPOSITE: **Mummy of Merenptah, found in the tomb of Amenhotep II**

The blind harper Early travelers to the Valley of the Kings made copies of the scenes they saw decorating the walls of the tombs. Most of these, like this image from the tomb of Ramesses III, copied by members of Napoleon's expedition to Egypt in 1798, include a significant amount of western interpretation, but represent important records nonetheless.

explore the area further. When he first arrived, he noted about sixteen tombs that were generally known. Over the next few years, he discovered or rediscovered eight more tombs, including the spectacular sepulcher of Seti I (who reigned about 1294–1279 B.C.), the largest and most extensively decorated tomb in the valley.

The key to the hieroglyphic code was cracked in 1822 by Jean-François Champollion, a French scholar who had dedicated his short but productive life to this task. Once the ancient texts could be deciphered, the field of Egyptology was born, and a new breed of scholars brought their talents to bear on the secrets of the Valley of the Kings. One of these was John Gardiner Wilkinson, who spent a great deal of time copying texts and inscriptions in the royal tombs with the goal of developing a chronology and shedding light on the lives of the ancient kings and their subjects.

Other excavators and copyists of this era include James Burton, Robert Hay, and Champollion himself, who traveled in Egypt between 1828 and 1829. In addition to the excellent copies made by his team, he and his partner, the Italian Ippolito Rosellini, were responsible for cutting two beautiful scenes from the walls of the tomb of Seti I. As Nicholas Reeves puts it in his book on the Valley of the Kings, "The scholarly mining destined to damage so irreparably one of the most beautiful tombs of the Valley of the Kings was off to a flying start." The Germans put in their first major appearance under the leadership of Carl Richard Lepsius, whose team simultaneously recorded and pillaged the monuments of Egypt in the 1840s. Twenty-five tombs appear on their maps of the Valley of the Kings, twenty-one in the east valley and four in the west.

The next decade marked a watershed in the history of Egyptian archaeology. Auguste Mariette, an energetic and competent French scholar who had originally come to Egypt in a futile search for Coptic manuscripts, founded the Egyptian Antiquities Service, for the first time putting some power over Egyptian antiquities in the hands of the Egyptian government. Unfortunately, the Herculean task that Mariette undertook, namely to excavate all over Egypt and gather objects for an Egyptian collection, meant that the work carried out was often badly supervised and sketchily recorded. Much of it was also never published. Several new tombs in the Valley of the Kings seem to have been discovered during his tenure as head of the Antiquities Service, but we no longer know which these were.

Further explorations and epigraphic work in the royal tombs were carried out over the next two decades, but the next major discovery was made in the summer of 1871 by an Egyptian family called Abd al-Rassul. This family lived in a village called Qurna, which is located next to the Valley of the Kings. The villagers had a reputation for knowing about and stealing objects from tombs that no one else knew of; they then sold their finds on the flourishing antiquities market. I heard one of the many versions of this discovery from a member of the family. I met him many years ago when I was a young inspector on the west bank, working with a foreign expedition at the palace

of Amenhotep III at Malqata. According to this man, whose name was Sheikh Ali, Ahmed Abd al-Rassul was pasturing his goats in the rocky hills above Deir al-Bahari, the location of the mortuary temple of Hatshepsut, when one of his charges fell into a crevice. Following the sound of distressed bleating, Ahmed found that the goat had fallen down a shaft in the rock. When he lowered himself down by means of a rope, he found himself in a corridor filled with battered coffins. He brought his brothers Hussein and Mohamed to investigate, and they realized that the coffins contained royal mummies.

The Abd al-Rassul brothers kept their secret for almost ten years, only entering the tomb three times and selling mostly only minor artifacts on the black market, although there was at least one rumor circulating at the time about a royal mummy who seems to have been sold to some foreign ladies. But the word got out, and representatives and even consuls of foreign countries began to visit Luxor to buy artifacts and transport them to Europe. Objects of clearly royal origin began to appear outside Egypt. This generated suspicion, and an investigation was initiated by those who were in charge of the Antiquities Department at the time: Gaston Maspero, the director of the Antiquities Service; his assistant Emile Brugsch; the first Egyptian Egyptologist, Ahmed Pasha Kamal; and the director of the Qena police, Daoud Pasha. Maspero traveled to Luxor to aid the police with their inquiries, and discovered not only that the Abd al-Rassul family was involved, but that the vice-consul of England in Luxor had misused his diplomatic privileges to smuggle antiquities outside of the country.

On April 14 1881, Maspero sent the police in Luxor to capture Ahmed Abd al-Rassul. Brugsch supervised a police interrogation, in which Ahmed denied any knowledge of the royal cache. The authorities searched his house and found no incriminating evidence, but, although they had nothing concrete to go on, their suspicions were not completely allayed. They kept Ahmed in prison while they continued their inquiries. On April 7, Daoud Pasha called for an official investigation. All the people in Qurna, including the mayor, said that Ahmed Abd al-Rassul was a respectable man and that he was not involved in illegal excavations or the smuggling of antiquities.

After his release, Ahmed asked the members of the family for a larger share of the profits as a reward for his stoicism. The other brothers refused, but

Deir al-Bahari The mortuary temple of the female pharaoh Hatshepsut dominates the bay of cliffs at Deir al-Bahari. It was in the rocky hills surrounding this site that the Abd al-Rassul family stumbled across the bodies of many of the New Kingdom's most powerful kings.

the seed of dissension had been sown. On June 25, Mohamed, the eldest member of the family, decided that it was better to give up the secret than risk Ahmed's defection and went secretly to the Qena police. Daoud Pasha went to the location of the treasure and found more than 30 coffins, statutes, and other objects.

On June 27, Emile Brugsch and Ahmed Pasha Kamal went to Thebes, and on July 4, they were presented by Mohamed with wonderful objects of royal origin. On July 6, they entered the tomb for the first time, and found the royal

mummies, coffins, and furniture. Many of the most famous kings of the New Kingdom were there, including the king who began the fight against the Hyksos, Seqenenre Taa II, and his son Ahmose, as well as Amenhotep I, Thutmosis I, II, and III, Seti I, Ramesses II, and Ramesses III. The coffin of Ramesses I was there, but the mummy was missing.

A royal mummy that ended up in the United States, in a museum at Niagara Falls, was recently identified as this last king; although this identification is not one hundred percent certain, it is extremely likely to be correct. The mummy was bought several years ago by Emory Museum in Atlanta, and recently returned to Egypt, a gift from the city of Atlanta to the Egyptian government. The return of this king, whether he is Ramesses I or not, was a great event, and an important symbol of the best kind of cooperation between nations.

In the space of only two days, the tomb was cleared and the mummies and their associated artifacts prepared for transport under the supervision of Brugsch, Mohamed Bek, the police director, and Ahmed Pasha Kamal. Some of the coffins were so heavy that they needed a dozen men to move them from their tomb in the valley to the banks of the Nile. On July 15, 1881, a steamer arrived to take the mummies and their trappings to Cairo.

On the day that the royal mummies departed, the people of Luxor lined the banks of the river to mourn for their ancestors. The women wore black and cried and the men stood stoically as they watched the great kings and queens from the past sail away to the Boulaq Museum in Cairo. This scene is beautifully recreated in a great Egyptian movie directed by Shadi Abdel Salam, starring Nadia Loutfi, called *The Night of Counting the Years*; better known to the public as *The Mummy*. When the boat carrying the royal corpses reached customs in Cairo, the inspector in charge could not find an entry for mummy in his register, so the great kings of Egypt entered the city as salted fish.

OPPOSITE: **Burial Chamber of Amenhotep II** In 1898, Victor Loret, then head of the Antiquities Service, discovered this tomb. In addition to the mummy of Amenhotep II himself, nine kings, as well as several still unidentified mummies, were entombed here. FOLLOWING PAGES: **Scene of mourning from the tomb of Ramose** Images of the funeral were included in the decoration of Egyptian tombs from the Old Kingdom on. This image conveys the grief felt by the family of this powerful vizier, as his mummy was taken to its final resting place.

The second cache of royal mummies was found in 1898 by the French archaeologist Victor Loret in the tomb of Amenhotep II, reputedly with a tip from Mohamed Abd al-Rassul. Loret found twelve of the mummies of royal kings such as Amenhotep II himself, Thutmosis IV, Merenptah, and many of the Ramesside kings. In a side chamber of this tomb were three unlabelled mummies that have been the subject of much scrutiny and debate. One is of a woman who was nicknamed 'the Elder Lady' by the first scholar to study the mummies; as discussed above, she has been identified with Queen Tiye; it has also been suggested that she is Nefertiti. The second mummy is of a young boy, to whom little attention has been paid.

The third mummy here is currently the center of a controversy. It has usually been assumed to be a young woman, but has also been identified on several occasions as a young man. Several Egyptologists over the years have suggested that the body might be that of Nefertiti, the great queen of Akhenaten and possibly pharaoh in her own right, but this theory has generally been dismissed for a number of reasons. The principal objection, aside from the ambiguity of the mummy's gender, is its age. Although there is some margin of error in the estimation of the age (the mummy of Amenhotep III, who must have been at least in his late forties when he died, looks to be about thirty-five), the mummy is young, probably about eighteen, with a maximum age of twenty-five. Nefertiti had already borne three of her six daughters when her husband came to the throne, and thus must have been at least in her mid-teens when he began his seventeen-year reign. This would have made her over thirty when she died.

I have long been against the use of DNA testing on Egyptian mummies, and have refused permission for samples to be taken for this purpose. DNA decays over time, and scientific experts in the field have advised me that it is very difficult, in the current state of the technology, to get a sample large enough to provide accurate results. Most of the results that have been obtained so far are likely to be the products of contamination. I did give permission to the laboratory of the Supreme Council of Antiquities to run a chromosome test on the mystery mummy: the lab found y-chromosomes present in the bone sample that they took, indicating that the mummy is, in fact, male. If these results are confirmed, the Nefertiti theory will be laid to rest forever, and we will have a new puzzle to solve.

In 1899, a fascinating shaft tomb was discovered in the royal valley by Loret. This lay near the tomb of Amenhotep II, and is now numbered KV36. This was partly intact, and still contained a significant number of funerary furnishings but was unfortunately never properly published, so remains incompletely understood. It belonged to a royal fan-bearer and child of the royal nursery named Maiherpri, who probably lived during the reign of Thutmosis IV.

This young man, who seems to have been about twenty-four when he died, is shown with a black face in the copy of the Book of the Dead that was buried with him, and his mummy seems to be of a person of mixed blood. An attempt had been made to strip the body of its amulets, at least the most valuable ones, but it was still covered by a funerary mask and laid within two nested anthropoid coffins and a rectangular outer shrine of wood. There was a third anthropoid coffin left in the center of the chamber; this should have been the innermost coffin, but had been abandoned because it was too big to fit inside the others.

Included in the finds from within the tombs was a canopic chest with four canopic jars, a game, complete with box and pieces, two quivers and seventy-five arrows, vessels of glass, faience, and stone, two dog collars, and offerings of meat, bread, and plants.

ABOVE: **Collar of a dog** Pets in ancient Egypt were very important to their masters; dogs are some of the first and most common domesticated animals shown with ancient Egyptian nobles. This dog collar was found in the tomb of Maiherpri in the Valley of the Kings.

CHAPTER EIGHT

WORK UNDER THEODORE DAVIS

A RICH AMERICAN BUSINESSMAN NAMED THEODORE DAVIS HELD the concession to the Valley of the Kings from 1902 to 1914. His attention had been called to the area by Howard Carter, who was chief inspector of the Theban area at the time. The plan was that Davis would fund Carter's work in the valley, in return for which the Antiquities Service, in the tradition of the day, would give Davis any duplicate artifacts that turned up. Carter had hoped to find the tomb of Thutmosis IV, and began work in January 1902. Unearthing this tomb took a year of work, over the course of which he made a number of interesting finds, including two small tombs and a wooden box containing two elaborate leather loincloths that had once belonged to Maiherpri. But finally Carter found the royal tomb for which he had been searching. On January 18, two hollows in the rock that held foundation deposits appeared, and then a stairway that led to the tomb of Thutmosis IV.

Davis, of course, was very pleased, and Carter convinced him that they should next look at a tomb known as KV20, which had been known for many years but had never been properly examined. The clearance of this tomb, which was filled with solidified debris that had been left behind by flooding over the millennia and evidently smelled terrible, was very difficult. But it was worth the work: Carter discovered enough royally inscribed material to assign it to Hatshepsut. Later analysis (by John Romer, in 1974) has demonstrated that KV20 was not originally built for this ruling queen, but instead was most likely the tomb carved by Ineni's men for Thutmosis I, and thus quite possibly the first tomb in the valley.

OPPOSITE: **Gold mask for a fetus**

In 1904, Carter was appointed chief inspector in the north of Egypt, and the new Chief Inspector of Luxor, James Quibell, took over as Davis's excavator. Less than a year later, Quibell and Davis discovered the tomb of Tutankhamun's great-grandparents (or grandparents, if Amenhotep III was his father), Yuya and Tjuya. If it had not been for the discovery of Tutankhamun's tomb, the tomb of Yuya and Tjuya would have been considered the most spectacular discovery from the Valley of the Kings. When found, the entrance to the stairways and descending corridors that led to the Burial Chamber was covered with limestone chips produced when two later tombs that lay nearby were carved from the rock. These later tombs were Twentieth Dynasty in date, so it was clear that the tomb dated to the Eighteenth or Nineteenth Dynasty. The outer doorway was still sealed with stone overlaid by mud plaster that bore the stamps of the necropolis: nine prostrate captives surmounted by the symbol of the mortuary god Anubis, a jackal. An opening in the top right-hand corner told the excavators that the tomb was not completely intact, but the existence of the blocking told them that most of the larger items of burial equipment might still be inside.

The corridor beyond this door was mostly empty. At the end was a second blocked doorway, again breached by a thieves' hole that had been hastily repaired. When the excavators cleared the later repair and peered through the gap in the plaster, they saw a chamber filled with elegant furniture. It was described by the archaeologist Arthur Weigall (quoted in Reeves, *The Complete Valley of the Kings*, p. 175): "Imagine entering a town house with had been closed for the summer; imagine the stuffy room, the stiff, silent appearance of the furniture, the feeling that some ghostly occupants of the vacant chairs have just been disturbed, the desire to throw open the windows to let life into the room once more."

Although the original excavators thought that only one group of thieves had entered the tomb, it is now believed that there were either two or three occasions on which the tomb was violated. Everything that could be carried away easily was gone: all the jewelry except what was inside the mummy wrappings, other metals, perfumes, and cosmetics. The objects that remained behind had been tossed about—the mummies had been poked and prodded and boxes lay with their lids ripped off. The missing perfumes and cosmetics pointed to

robbery soon after the burial, since these goods would not have lasted for long. Intrusive sealings dating to the reign of Ramesses III suggest that the tomb was entered again in this period; either at the same time or later, some attempt was made to straighten up a bit before the tomb was hastily closed.

But what remained intact was still spectacular. The centerpieces were the coffins of Yuya and Tjuya themselves, and their wonderfully preserved mummies. There were canopic chests, shabtis, chairs, beds, a wig and a wig basket, sandals, a mirror, vessels of stone and pottery, amulets and scarabs, and even Yuya's chariot, among other things. It was a spectacular find, and provided a great deal of fascinating information on the family of Tiye.

After the discovery of this tomb, Quibell and Davis (who was, by all accounts, a very difficult man to work with and for) had a falling out; Arthur Weigall stepped in briefly before an experienced excavator named Edward Ayrton took his place. Ayrton was very thorough and methodical, and he made a number of important discoveries.

These discoveries included many interesting small finds and the tombs of Horemheb; a late Nineteenth Dynasty king named Siptah; a number of private tombs; and the mysterious tomb KV55, holding what may be the body of Akhenaten (see above).

Included in these discoveries were tantalizing traces of Tutankhamun himself. In the winter of 1906, Ayrton found a small faience cup inscribed with the name of Tutankhamun

Anthropoid coffin of Tjuya Mother of Tiye and grandmother of Akhenaten, Tjuya was buried with her husband in the Valley of the Kings, a high honor for non-royalty. Inside this coffin, which was nested inside two outer coffins, was Tjuya's mummy, adorned with gilded linen and a stucco mask.

Cylindrical libation vase. A number of faience vessels were found in the tomb of Thutmosis IV. On the front of this example are the cartouches of the king himself.

a dozen feet below surface level, unassociated with any architectural features. In 1907, within a shaft in the same area, he excavated a small pit containing different types of pottery vessels, one of them a beautiful wine jar with a long neck. Some of these vessels were stamped with an official necropolis seal and inscribed with the name of Tutankhamun, called 'one who is loved by the gods.' Also in the shaft was a vessel covered with a piece of material inscribed with the name of Tutankhamun, dated to the sixth year of his reign.

Working with Davis, who, among his other flaws, refused to publish properly, proved eventually to be too much for Ayrton. In 1908, he not only resigned from his position but left Egyptology for good. Davis, hired a young man named Ernest Harold Jones in Ayrton's stead. But Jones found little of major importance (by the standards of the time). He did uncover, in 1909, a small undecorated rock-cut chamber whose contents included several pieces of gold foil (from chariot fittings), one decorated with a scene of Tutankhamun shooting arrows at a copper target and others bearing the names of Ay; and an alabaster shabti. Jones, who was tubercular, died in 1911. He was replaced by Harry Burton, who attempted clearance of several tombs, but again made no major finds.

Davis decided that the rock-cut chamber found by Jones was the tomb of Tutankhamun, or at least what remained of it. A theory current at the time was that the tomb of this king lay somewhere near the tomb of Amenhotep III and had been destroyed by Horemheb. Loyal priests then collected the materials and hid them away. In fact, the material in this small chamber probably originated in the tomb of Ay. Nonetheless Davis, convinced that his quest was over, gave up the concession to the Valley of the Kings in 1912; he died soon afterward, never knowing the riches that he had, by a margin of about six feet, just missed uncovering.

OPPOSITE: **Dummy vases of Yuya and Tjuya** These limestone vases have been painted to imitate various types of hard stone. They are solid pieces, with no openings or interior spaces.

CHAPTER NINE

HOWARD CARTER AND LORD CARNARVON

H OWARD CARTER, WHO WAS NEVER FORMALLY TRAINED AS AN Egyptologist, became one of the most famous archaeologists ever known. Born May 9, 1874 in London, England, he was the youngest son of eleven children. He was sickly and apparently rather spoiled as a child. His father, Samuel John Carter, was a talented and successful artist. Howard had little formal schooling, but was trained by his father in the techniques of drawing and was working as an artist at an early age.

When Carter was seventeen, Lord Amherst, who was fascinated by ancient Egypt and had an important collection of Egyptian artifacts, introduced him to the English archaeologist Percy Newberry. At the time, Newberry was working for the Egypt Exploration Fund, a society of wealthy Egyptological patrons who sponsored many important expeditions to Egypt. After a brief internship at the British Museum, Carter was hired to go with Newberry to Middle Egypt to copy scenes and texts in some rock-cut tombs at Beni Hasan. Apparently of a very logical and methodical turn of mind, Carter did not approve of the techniques that were being used by the expedition, in which the paintings were traced in outline and then inked in with solid black back in England by people who usually knew nothing of the subject matter. Fortunately (or unfortunately!), most of this work had already been done; the young artist was asked to make detailed watercolors of selected figures and hieroglyphs, which he did beautifully. After Beni Hasan, Carter went with Newberry to the nearby site of Bersheh,

OPPOSITE: **Howard Carter**

where he had to chance to make the sort of copies he wanted, outlining the figures and adding interior detail whenever possible. This technique became standard for epigraphy in Egypt.

That same year, Carter was sent to work with the famous British archaeologist, William Flinders Petrie, now known as the Father of Egyptology, at Tell al-Amarna. Petrie didn't think much of him at first, and Carter was not impressed by the living conditions. The day after he arrived, he was told to build his own room out of mud brick and given a month's supply of tinned food (the tins of which were to be used for the storage of artifacts). But he took to the work, and Petrie rapidly became impressed with his intelligence and abilities.

In 1892, Carter's father died, which was a great blow, and he fell ill as a result, missing much of the season. After he recovered, he went back to Beni Hasan with Newberry, then to several other sites around Egypt. The Egypt Exploration Fund was pleased with his work, an in 1893, he was appointed artist to Edouard Naville at Deir al-Bahari. He spend six years here, helping to excavate, reconstruct, and record the temple of Hatshepsut, and emerged a well-trained archaeologist and Egyptologist. Although he was an excellent artist and a highly competent photographer, he discovered that what he really wanted to do was excavate.

In 1899, the head of the Antiquities Service, Gaston Maspero, appointed him chief inspector of monuments in Upper Egypt. He made his first important discovery on a rainy evening in 1900, as he was riding his horse home through the Theban hills. Suddenly, one of the legs of his horse fell into a hole, which turned out to be the entrance to an ancient burial. He was not able to excavate until a year later, but when he did, he discovered a chamber associated with the mortuary complex of King Nebhepetre Mentuhotep, first ruler of the Middle Kingdom; he nicknamed this tomb the Bab al-Hosan (the Gate of the Horse). Expecting a major find, perhaps even an intact royal tomb, Carter invited some important dignitaries to the opening of the tomb. But inside the chamber was only an empty, uninscribed coffin; a shaft containing three wooden boats and some pottery vessels; and a magnificent statue of the king, which is now at the Egyptian Museum. The dignitaries were disappointed, and Carter decided that in future he would

check out his discoveries carefully first by himself before inviting any VIPs to come and see them.

Carter was occupied from 1902 to 1904 by his duties as chief inspector of Upper Egypt and excavator for Theodore Davis. At that time, he moved nine mummies from the tomb of Amenhotep II to the Cairo Museum, leaving three unidentified mummies in situ. After his transfer in 1904 to Saqqara in the north, his luck changed for a while. In 1905, he got into an altercation with a group of drunk and unruly French tourists, who filed a complaint with Carter's higher-ups in the Antiquities Service. Carter was asked to apologize, but refused and was forced to resign. He spent the next few months cobbling together a meager living by painting watercolors and doing some archaeological drawings.

Lord Carnarvon was a wealthy Englishman who had come to Egypt for his health in 1903. Several years earlier, he had been involved in a car accident (in one of the first cars) from which he had never recovered fully. To avoid the bitter English winter, he set up residence at Aswan, where many English lords came for three months a year. But Carnarvon found the slow pace of life there dull, and turned his attention to antiquities. With the help of Lord Cromer, the British Consul-General, he got a concession to work in the area of Sheikh Abdel Qurna in Luxor. He enjoyed the work (his part of which was sitting inside a tent of mosquito netting, drinking tea), even though not much was found, and wisely decided that he needed the help of an expert. The head of the Antiquities Service, Gaston Maspero, who liked and

Statue of Mentuhotep Carter's first great discovery was a chamber beneath the mortuary temple of Mentuhotep II, founder of the Middle Kingdom, at Deir al-Bahari. It contained an empty coffin, some wooden boats, and this massive statue of the king in the red crown of Lower Egypt.

believed in Carter, introduced him to Lord Carnarvon in 1905. For the next ten years, Carter worked as Lord Carnarvon's representative at various sites, primarily in the Theban area, but also at Sakha and Tell Balamun in the Nile Delta. They made some interesting discoveries, including a number of decorated private tombs. Carter also acted as a middleman for Carnarvon and other collectors involved in the antiquities trade, using his superb eye to choose spectacular artifacts for his patrons.

Carter had long wanted to return to the Valley of the Kings, where he was sure Tutankhamun's tomb still lay, hidden and possibly intact. He knew that the body of this king had not been found in either royal cache, and was convinced that the materials found by Davis were associated in some way with his still undiscovered tomb. It must, he was sure, lie nearby. Once Davis gave up his concession to the area, the field was clear for Carter. It was only a matter of convincing Lord Carnarvon that it was their destiny to find this tomb, which he did successfully.

Carter and Carnarvon's first season in the valley took place in 1915, when they re-explored the tomb of Amenhotep III. This lay in the western arm of the valley, and had never been fully cleared. The tomb had been fairly thoroughly robbed in antiquity, but Carter did find some foundation deposits, part of a shabti of Queen Tiye, a fragment of the king's canopic chest, and, in the well shaft, the hub of a chariot wheel and part of a bracelet.

In December 1917, Carter and Carnarvon were granted the concession to the main valley, and they began their search for the golden tomb. Carter was a smart archaeologist. We say that some archaeologists can smell the past; this was definitely true of Carter. He was also lucky: He was well funded by Lord Carnarvon, and was thus able to hire one hundred workmen at a time to remove the sand, dirt, and stone rubble from the valley. His plan was to excavate the valley down to the bedrock, and he drove his men hard. The workmen would have gotten up early in the morning, organized and directed by their *reis* (overseer), and labored hard all day. As Egyptian excavation teams still do, they sang together to make their day joyful and pleasant. Carter would have spent much of his time in his tent, thinking and studying the artifacts that had been collected. Based on the evidence found by Davis, he decided to concentrate his work between the tombs of Ramesses IX and Ramesses VI.

The seasons between 1917 and 1922 were lean, with little of interest emerging from the sands of the valley. Carter was still sure that he would make a major discovery, but Lord Carnarvon began to lose interest. He did not like visiting the valley because of its darkness at night and the snakes that he saw during the day. In the summer of 1922, he called Carter to his home in England, Highclere, and told him that they were finished. But Carter was sure that they were on the verge of a great discovery, and convinced him to fund one more season.

The team arrived in the valley at the end of October 1922. Carter brought with him a canary from England, to give them all luck. Work began in the only area left uncleared, below the tomb of Ramesses VI. Carter had been avoiding this area because it would have inconvenienced tourists to the tomb above, but it was now the only place left to look. He told his workmen to record the Ramesside huts that lay there, and then to sink a trench right through them. We can imagine the three days and nights that passed, as Carter knew he was using up his last chance to find the tomb. Perhaps he thought about Carnarvon, who might change his mind and stop the excavations at any time. We cannot know how he felt, but I am sure that it did not come to his mind that the morning of November 4, 1922, would be his moment of glory.

Guardian statue This statue was one of a pair found flanking the entrance to Tutankhamun's burial chamber. Both were made of wood covered with bitumen, with details like headdresses, kilts, and sandals covered with gold leaf.

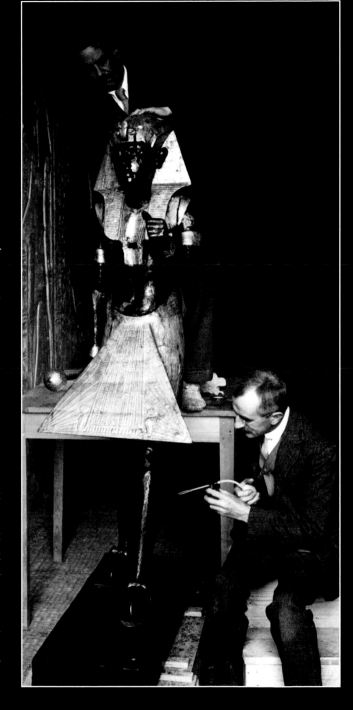

CHAPTER TEN

THE TOMB OF TUTANKHAMUN

THERE ARE SEVERAL DIFFERENT VERSIONS OF THE DISCOVERY OF the tomb of Tutankhamun. According to one, Carter arrived at the excavation in the early morning of November 4 and found that the atmosphere at the site had changed. Everyone was quiet. No one was singing and there was a look of expectation on everyone's faces. A waterboy had dug a hole in which to set his jars of water, and come across the top of a step cut into the rock. The workmen cleared away some sand, and found that it was the beginning of a stairway. Carter directed his workmen to remove more sand and found a flight of fifteen steps, each about 1.60 meters wide and 4 meters deep. The men and boys worked all day, and by the evening had found that the stairs led to a doorway blocked with stones and plaster. Stamped all over the plaster surface of the wall was the Jackal-and-Nine-Captive seal of the royal cemetery. At first Carter thought that the tomb, or cache (he was not sure at first which it was), was completely inviolate, but then he noticed an area in the upper left-hand corner that had been replastered and resealed. This indicated that the tomb had been entered before, but had been resecured in antiquity. It would not be completely intact, but might still hold great riches.

Carter sent a telegram to Lord Carnarvon saying: "At last we have made a wonderful discovery in the valley, a magnificent tomb with seals intact, recovered and waiting for your arrival: Congratulations!" Lord Carnarvon and his daughter, Lady Evelyn Herbert, came immediately, arriving at the Luxor station, where they were met by the governor and Carter, on November 23.

OPPOSITE: **Statue of the god Ptah from the tomb of Tutankhamun**

Once Carnarvon had arrived, clearance could begin in earnest. The stairwell was emptied, and the entire doorway became visible. Down at the bottom were more seal impressions, several of which bore the name of Tutankhamun. On November 25, just one day before the great unveiling, the workmen began to remove the plastered blocking of the tomb. Behind it they found a corridor cut in the rock, 7.6 meters long. It was full of dust and stone rubble, and led to another plastered doorway, covered again with necropolis seals, again bearing evidence that the tomb had been opened and officially reclosed in antiquity.

At 4 p.m. on November 26, Carter made a hole in the second plastered doorway and looked inside. Carnarvon stood by impatiently, anxious to know what was beyond the blocking. Carter lit a candle and peered into the opening. Carnarvon asked him: "What do you see?" Carter's reply was, "Wonderful things!" In his publication of the tomb, Carter describes the fateful moment thus, "At first I could see nothing, the hot air escaping from the chamber causing the candle flame to flicker, but presently as my eyes grew accustomed to the light, details of the room within emerged slowly from the mist. Strange animals, statues and gold, everywhere the glint of gold." Carter also wrote: "[It was] the most wonderful experience that I have ever lived through and certainly one whose like I can never hope to see again."

The official opening of the tomb was on November 29, 1922, and the next ten years witnessed the discovery of over five thousand artifacts, more than anyone had ever hoped for or expected, packed into four small rooms. An expert team was assembled, and many of the great English and American Egyptologists of the day were involved in one way or another. Carter's principal assistant at the beginning was Walter Mace, who was invaluable, but whose health was not good. He left Egypt in 1924 and died in 1928. Alfred Lucas, who worked as a chemist in the Antiquities Service, directed the conservation of the objects from the tomb. His book on Egyptian materials and techniques is still considered to be one of the finest on the subject. The chief photographer was Harry Burton, who had worked earlier with Theodore Davis. Sir Alan Gardiner, a great philologist who wrote a book on Egyptian grammar that is still used today, also worked closely with Carter. The great American Egyptologist Henry James Breasted, who became the first director of Chicago House in Luxor, also helped with the material from the tomb. These men were

View of the Antechamber, tomb of Tutankhamun The chambers of Tutankh-amun's tomb were crammed with thousands of objects. Each piece had to be carefully extracted from the spot where it lay without disturbing the objects nearby, recorded, and conserved. Carrying out this process for all the artifacts in the tomb took almost ten years.

joined by Carter's first mentor, Percy Newberry, Egyptologist and professor at the University of Liverpool, and his wife, and Americans Walter Hauser and Lindsey Foote Hall.

Clearance of the tomb took almost ten years. The nearby tomb of Ramesses XI was used as a storeroom, and the tomb of Seti II was used as a photo and conservation lab. Carter and his team worked carefully and methodically; the care with which each object was preserved and recorded stands as a tribute to their professionalism. This was fairly unusual, given the more usual techniques of the day. Contrast this, for example, with the two-day clearance of the Deir al-Bahari cache; most excavators of the period would have had everything out within a month or so.

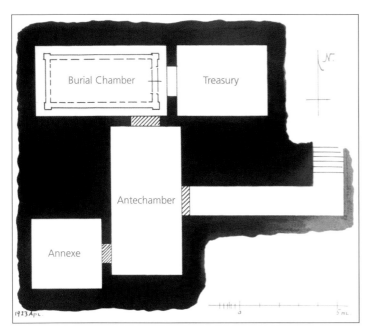

Plan of the tomb of
Tutankhamun

The tomb itself is relatively unimpressive by the royal standards of the Valley of the Kings, comprising only four small rooms. The doorway at the end of the first corridor leads into an Antechamber cut, like all the rooms of the tomb, into the bedrock. This room gives direct access to two more chambers. A doorway in the south end of the western wall of the Antechamber leads to a chamber that was dubbed the Annexe (2.9 by 4 meters). A second doorway, located in the middle of the Antechamber's north wall and flanked by lifesize guardian statues, leads to the Burial Chamber itself (4.3 by 6.4 meters). At the northern end of the east wall of the Burial Chamber is the doorway into a storage chamber, called by the excavators the Treasury.

As discussed above, this would not have been the tomb originally planned for the king, but was most likely adapted hastily for the royal burial from a pre-existing private tomb. Its original layout may have corresponded to the tomb of Yuya and Tjuya.

The Corridor was filled with rubble, through which the tunnel that had been burrowed by tomb robbers and then refilled by the necropolis officials could be traced. Carter found a number of objects mixed in with this rubble, including stone and pottery vessels (some fragmentary), clay seals, some bronze razors, wooden labels, and many bits and pieces of wood, faience, glass, and metalwork that had most likely come from objects taken from the tomb. Also found here, according to Carter's records, was a beautiful limestone head of the king as the sun god Nefertem, rising from a lotus.

The Antechamber is 8 meters long. Thieves had entered this room twice and had moved many artifacts from their original locations. It was crowded with pieces, large and small, all jumbled together in ways that made them hard to extricate from one another. Carter recorded in his diary that this room contained 171 major artifacts; there were 600 to 700 objects all together, which took

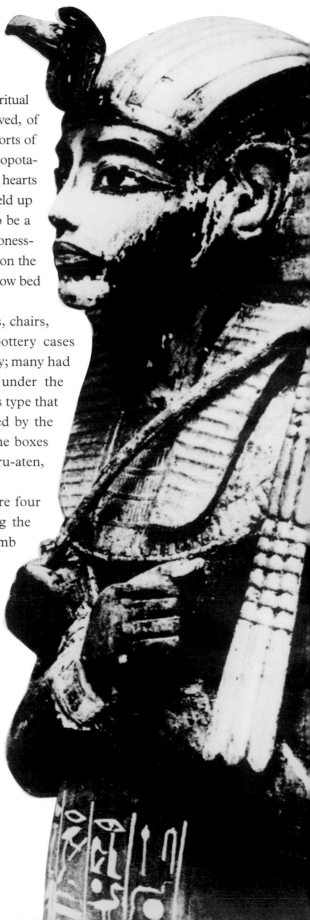

almost two months to clear. Against the west wall were three ritual couches supported by fantastic animals, wonderfully preserved, of gilded wood with composite inlays of ivory or glass. The supports of one couch were in the form of the goddess Anmut—part hippopotamus, part crocodile, and part lioness—who would devour the hearts of the unworthy, causing them to die forever. Another was held up by two cows with the sun disk between her horns, thought to be a goddess named Mehetweret. The third couch was borne by lionesses. It is interesting to note that, judging from the inscriptions on the side rails, whoever put the couches together got pieces of the cow bed and the lioness bed mixed up.

Piled on top and stacked beneath the couches were boxes, chairs, stools, and other smaller objects, including many oval pottery cases containing meat. All of the boxes had been rifled in antiquity; many had been hastily repacked and reclosed. One of the boxes under the lioness bed was a portable carrying chest, the only one of its type that has survived from ancient times. Another held a staff used by the young king, and many other important pieces. Some of the boxes bore other royal names, including Akhenaten, Neferneferu-aten, and Meritaten.

Against the south and east walls of the Antechamber were four dismantled chariots that had been badly damaged during the robberies and were only able to be extracted from the tomb and reconstructed through painstaking work by Carter and his team. The two most elaborate of these were of gilded wood with inlays of glass and stone; these were identified by Carter as state chariots. With the chariots were yokes, harnesses, blinkers, whip-stocks, and other related items.

Shabti of King Tutankhamun This funerary statuette of Tutankhamun shows the king in the nemes headdress, adorned at the brow with the protective images of a cobra and vulture. The figure still holds a flail, but its crook is missing. FOLLOWING PAGES: **View from the Antechamber to the Burial Chamber** Here the two guardian statues can be seen flanking the entrance to the Burial Chamber, which was still plastered over when Carter found it.

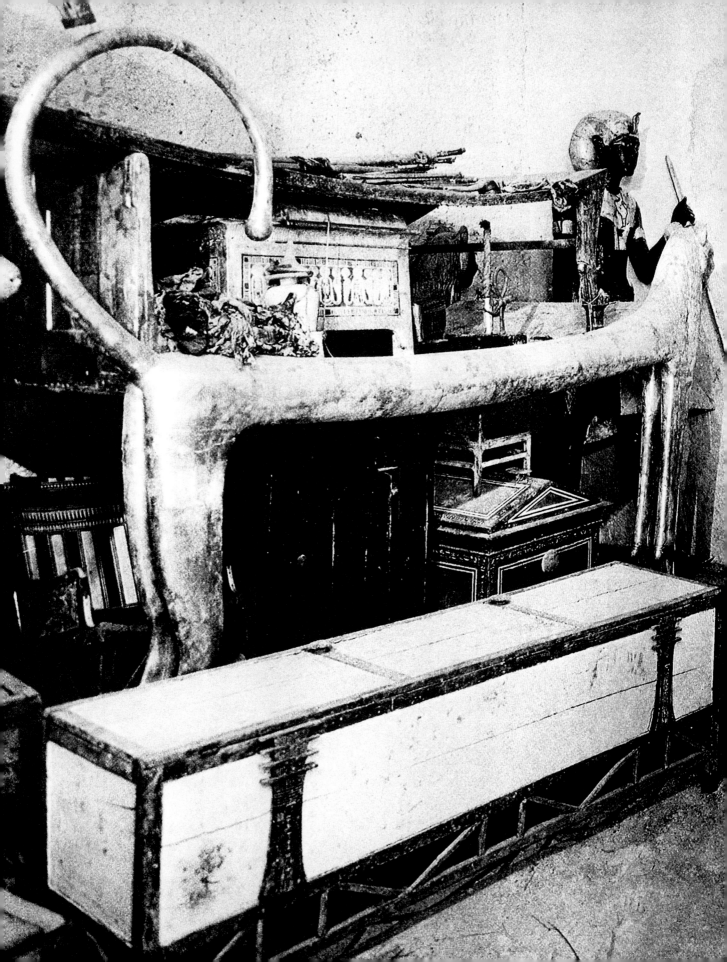

The doorway in the center of the north wall had been plastered closed. The blocking was flanked by two life-size statues of the king, wearing the bag wig—one type of royal headdress—on one side and the *nemes* headdress on the other. The second statue is labeled as the king's ka. When Carter first saw these images, they were shrouded in linen shawls. Each is of wood, its skin painted black—a color associated with fertility and rebirth—with a thick resin. The kilts, headdresses, and staffs were plastered and gilded. Hollows inside the statues were probably meant to hold rolls of papyrus, but these were missing.

The other particularly important piece found here, on the floor near one of the statues was a large painted box that held clothing evidently worn by Tutankhamun as a child. It has been nicknamed the 'Hunting Box' because of the scenes painted on its sides and vaulted lid, which show the king hunting desert game and in battle against the Syrians on one side and the Nubians on the other.

The excavator believed that this room was a magazine, because a number of the items found inside bore the names of other kings, including Akhenaten, Thutmosis III, Smenkhkare, and Amenhotep III.

Carter at work Here Carter and one of his workmen examine a coffin of Tutankhamun. **FOLLOWING PAGES: Innermost coffin of Tutankhamun** The golden king was buried in a nest of coffins. Inside the outer stone sarcophagus were three smaller receptacles, each inside the other. Inside this solid gold coffin was the mummy of the king himself.

Mirror case in the form of an ankh The word for mirror in ancient Egyptian was *ankh* (which also meant 'life'), making this ankh-shaped mirror case an appropriate receptacle. The interior of this piece is coated with silver, thus the lid itself also could have functioned as a reflective surface.

The Burial Chamber. On February 17, 1923, Carter removed the blocking from the doorway between the Antechamber and the room to the west. He found himself face-to-face with a huge golden shrine, 6.4 meters long and 4 meters wide, that filled the entire room with only a narrow space of less than a meter around it. The shrine was like the outer part of a Russian doll: Inside the shrine were nested three smaller shrines, all of gilded wood, protecting a rectangular quartzite sarcophagus decorated with figures of four winged goddesses, their arms outstretched to protect the king. Three anthropoid coffins were nested inside this massive coffin of stone, the first two of gilded wood and the innermost of solid gold, 2.5 to 3.5 millimeters. thick and weighing 111.04 kilograms, with silver handles. The coffins fitted together with barely a centimeter to spare. The three inner coffins and the mummy sat on a low bed made of solid wood with the feet and head of a lion. The weight of all the coffins together was 137.5 kilograms. Various objects, including eleven magical oars, an Anubis fetish (an animal skin filled with embalming solution), several boxes, several wine jars, and two alabaster lamps were found in the narrow space left around the outer shrine. A funerary bouquet of persea and olive lay where it had been left in a corner of the chamber.

The outer shrine had been breached, but the necropolis seal on the next was intact. This second shrine had been draped with a linen pall decked with flowers of gilded bronze; before its doors were two elaborately carved and painted perfume jars of alabaster. Other items lay between the walls of the nested shrines: bows and quivers full of arrows, sticks, staffs, and fans, among other things. The outer sarcophagus was opened on February 12, 1924, but it was not until the following season, on October 10, 1925, that the team opened the first coffin. On top of the second coffin was a linen shroud and the remains of garlands of flowers, left by the hands of the king's loved ones or priests. On October 23, the second coffin was opened and the third, again covered by a linen pall and floral garlands, was revealed.

On October 28, 1925, the lid of the third and final coffin was lifted and the beautiful gold mask, with its inlays of lapis lazuli, carnelian, quartz, obsidian,

OPPOSITE: **Broad collar with falcon heads** Many fabulous pieces of jewelry were found in the tomb of Tutankhamun. This broad collar is made of gold and colored glass.

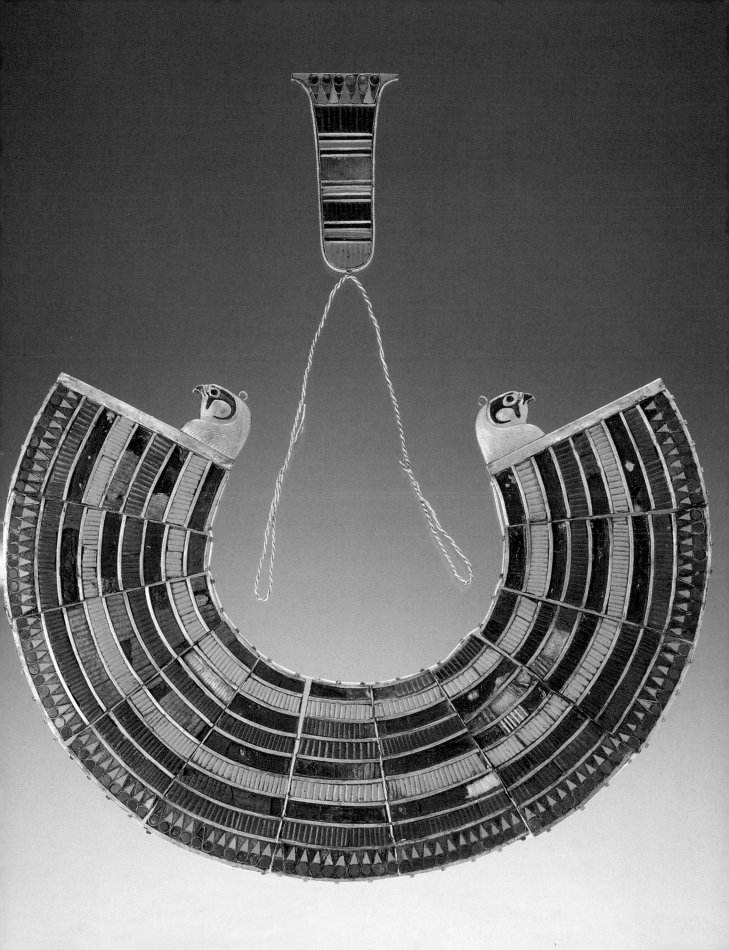

turquoise, and glass, that lay over the face of the mummy appeared to the astonished excavators. This funerary mask, in which the king wears the *nemes* headdress surmounted by the cobra and vulture goddesses, the braided and curled beard of divinity, and a broad collar, is one of the greatest masterpieces of Egyptian art. Few photographs show the back of this mask; it is inscribed with a religious text.

The ancient priests had poured a great deal of resin over the royal body, causing both the mummy and its mask to stick to the coffin. This made it extremely difficult to examine the body. The autopsy team, composed of Douglas Derry from the Egyptian University in Cairo and Saleh Bey Hamdi of Alexandria, worked on the mummy within its coffin. The unwrapping began on November 11, 1925, and the team found the body in poor condition, primarily as a result of the excessive libations with which it had been covered. There were more than one hundred objects wrapped with the mummy, a majority of which were of gold. As mentioned above, these included amulets; necklaces of various sorts; bracelets; finger and toe stalls; and two daggers, one of iron.

In order to lift the body from the coffin, the excavators cut it into large pieces and reassembled it in a tray of sand. The head was stuck inside the mask, and required the careful use of hot knives for extraction. A bead-work cap covered the shaved skull of the pharaoh, whose age was estimated at eighteen. The height of mummy was 1.63 meters; Derry suggested that Tutankhamun's original height was 1.67 meters. The autopsy team was not able to propose a cause of death.

OPPOSITE LEFT: **Tutankhamun in the red crown** Found in the Treasury with a number of other figures of the young king in various costumes and poses, this statuette represents Tutankhamun in the red crown of Lower Egypt, holding a curved staff and a flail.

OPPOSITE RIGHT: **Pectoral with winged scarab** This pectoral, of lapis lazuli, gold, and other precious materials, forms a clever rebus of the king's throne name, Nebkheperure. The semicircle at the bottom is a basket, representing neb; the scarab in the center is the sign for kheper, with plural strokes below to form kheperu; and the sun disk above symbolizes the sun god, Re.

The Treasury. To the north of the Burial Chamber was a smaller room dubbed by the excavators the Treasury. This had also been entered by thieves, who would have had to squeeze around the shrines in the Burial Chamber to gain access to it. The entrance to the room was guarded by a life-size figure of the god Anubis in the form of a jackal, lying upon a shrine. Against the north wall was a square shrine of gilded wood, its sides protected by beautiful free-standing carved images of four protective goddesses (Isis, Nephthys, Neith, and Selket), the whole set upon a gilded sledge. Nested inside was a canopic chest made of Egyptian alabaster, the four stoppers in the shape of the head of the king wearing a *nemes* headdress. The canopic material was inside this chest, each of the four packages wrapped carefully and placed inside a golden coffinette.

On one side of the room was a row of ivory and wooden boxes which had once held jewelry; much of this was found thrown about outside by the robbers. On the other side were a number of shrines which held wooden statues of the king and a number of gods. Three of these beautiful images represent Tutankhamun himself, in one case walking, holding a staff and a flail, in another riding on the back of a leopard or panther, and in the third on a papyrus skiff, holding a harpoon. Many model boats had been set atop the boxes and shrines; there were over thirty of these. Two more chariots, identified as hunting chariots by Carter, lay in a tangle in one corner. Also in this chamber, carefully mummified and placed in their own coffins, were the two still-born children of the king and his young queen.

The Annexe. The western door from the Ante-chamber led into a room dubbed the Annexe. This room had also been disturbed by robbers and put back into a semblance of order by the necropolis police. It was crammed with over two thousand objects. Among the objects found in the room were about thirty-six wine or beer jars, closed with mud seals. The great philologists James Breasted and Sir Alan Gardiner studied the seals found in this room carefully, and deter-

mined that most were labeled with Year 9 of the reign of Tutankhamun. Recently, scientists in England studied the remains of these jars and determined that Egyptian beer had a higher alcohol content than today's beer. The Treasury also contained more boats, furniture, including a bed, chairs, and stools, and many baskets.

Although some shabti figures were found in the Treasury, most were discovered in the Annexe. They are made of all sorts of materials: wood, various types of stone, and colored faience, and wear many different headdresses and wigs. Six of the largest had been given to the king by his high officials Nakhtmin and Maya; it is possible that others were gifts to the king from other important courtiers.

The Decoration of the Tomb. Due most likely to the short time available for the preparation of the tomb, only the Burial Chamber was decorated. Its walls were covered with a thick layer of mortar, on top of which was applied a background of golden yellow. The style of the scenes shows clearly the influence of the Amarna period: The figures are short, with sagging bellies and large, almond shaped eyes. The scenes here were designed to help insure the successful transition of the king to the afterlife and guarantee his continual survival for eternity.

The entrance to the chamber is in the eastern part of the south wall. The western half of this wall is occupied by a scene showing the king wearing a bag wig and standing between the goddess Hathor, who offers him an ankh, the sign of life, and the mortuary god Anubis, who stands with one hand on the shoulder of the king and an ankh in the other. Behind Anubis stands Isis, who greets the king with a special gesture (known as the *Ny-ny*); this ritual was meant to welcome the king to the netherworld with pure, sacred water. Also on this wall are three minor deities of the Duat, the ancient Egyptian netherworld.

ABOVE: **Senet game** A number of game boards were found in Tutankhamun's tomb. This elegant example is made of ebony and ivory; the tiny pieces with which the game was played were found still stored inside the attached drawer.

West wall of the Burial Chamber The west wall, ultimate focus of the cult, is decorated with a scene from the Book of the Dead.

The eastern wall of the chamber is decorated with scenes depicting the king's funeral. The mummiform coffin of the king lies on a canopied bed inside a shrine that is in turn on board a boat pulled on a sledge by the king's courtiers. As they pull, the nobles speak, welcoming the king in peace to the west. Above the king's mummy was written: "The good god, Lord of the Two Lands, Nebkheperure, given life for eternity." Small figures of Isis and Nephthys protect the royal shrine and the mummy within.

The west wall was the most important wall in the tomb, the primary focus of the cult. The west was the location of the netherworld, the place where the sun set at night so that it could be reborn in the morning. In Tutankhamun's tomb, this wall was dedicated to a chapter from the Book of What is in the Underworld (often called the Book of the Dead). On the top register is the solar bark in which Khepri, the scarab beetle who represents the rising sun, is given homage by two figures of Osiris. Before the bark are five standing gods, including Maat and Horus. The wall below this register is divided into

twelve boxes, each containing a baboon representing one of the twelve hours of the night. The king had to travel through these hours, which were fraught with danger, before he and the sun could be reborn in the morning.

There are three separate vignettes on the northern wall of the Burial Chamber. The first shows Ay wearing the blue crown—the war helmet worn by the heir to the throne— and the leopard skin of a sem priest as he performs the ritual of the opening of the mouth on the Osiriform mummy of Tutankhamun. This was the rite by which the body of the king was prepared to receive offerings in the afterlife. The next scene shows Nut, goddess of the sky, giving, like Hathor on the east wall, the *Ny-ny* greeting to a standing figure of Tutankh-amun, now transformed into an effective being in the afterlife, holding a staff, a mace, and an ankh. The text above this scene promises the king life for eternity. The last scene on this wall depicts Tutankhamun embracing the god Osiris, lord of the Netherworld. Behind the king is his spiritual double, or ka; between the two arms of the ka sign that surmount the head of this figure is the Horus name of Tutankhamun: 'mighty bull.'

North wall of the Burial Chamber The scenes in the burial chamber were painted with tempera. The north wall depicts rites connected with the transformation of the king into a divine being.

CHAPTER ELEVEN

TROUBLE IN PARADISE: CARTER AND THE ANTIQUITIES SERVICE

THE DISCOVERY OF THE TUTANKHAMUN'S TOMB WAS TOUTED BY the press as the most important discovery of the twentieth century—the greatest find in the history of Egyptology. The newspapers claimed that the artifacts were worth millions of English pounds. The fact that the discovery had been funded by an English aristocrat added an extra element of allure to the event.

But archaeology is no different from any other field, and jealousy and infighting can happen. Although many people are unaware of this, the golden tomb of Tutankhamun was a battleground, a pawn in a struggle for power. Carter and Carnarvon began their work together during an era of foreign domination in Egypt and Egyptian archaeology. In most cases, finds were divided between the sponsor of the excavation and the Egyptian Antiquities Service, so the hope of taking home spectacular objects was usually a major impetus for funding. Foreign patrons liked to treat their discoveries as their own, to be shared perhaps with the Egyptians (who, in fact, had official control over all expeditions), but fundamentally belonging to the discoverer.

Carter and Carnarvon seem in many ways to have thought that the tomb was theirs to do with as they pleased. They did not even invite Pierre Lacau, then head of the Antiquities Service, to the official opening, and they completely ignored the Egyptian press. Carter and the Lord invited only an English reporter and friend of Carter's, Arthor Mirton, to the opening. The result was that the Egyptian Antiquities Service, who should have been the first in-formed, had to read the newspapers to find out the details of the discovery. It is almost as

OPPOSITE: **Head of Tutankhamun as the god Nefertem**

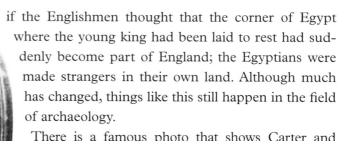

if the Englishmen thought that the corner of Egypt where the young king had been laid to rest had suddenly become part of England; the Egyptians were made strangers in their own land. Although much has changed, things like this still happen in the field of archaeology.

There is a famous photo that shows Carter and members of the Egyptian government, all smiling at the camera. One can only imagine what was behind the smiles. Arthur Mace, a member of Carter's team who was the assistant curator of the Metropolitan Museum of Art Egyptian Section and a relative of the famous English archaeologist Flinders Petrie, wrote a letter to his wife Winifred describing Luxor after the discovery. He wrote, "The atmosphere of Luxor is rather nerve-wracking at present. The Winter Palace is a scream. No one talks of anything but the tomb. Newspapermen swarm, and you daren't say a word without looking round everywhere to see if any one is listening. Some of them are trying to make mischief between Carnarvon and the Department of Antiquities, and all Luxor is taking sides one way or the other. Archaeology plus journalism is bad enough, but when you add politics, it becomes a little too much . . . ." Mace, as the co-author with Carter of the first volume published on the tomb, was very close to the center of the storm.

Carnarvon, having funded excavations in the royal valley for almost sixteen years, assumed that he would take home a good percentage of the artifacts. Twenty-four hours after the discovery, a judge ruled that Egyptian law permitted Carnarvon and Carter to take fifty percent of the artifacts. However, the Egyptian Antiquities Service announced that, since the tomb had been found intact, Antiquities law decreed that all of the finds were the property of the Egyptian government.

ABOVE: **George Herbert, Lord Carnarvon** Victim of an automobile accident as a young man, Carnarvon came to Egypt for his health, and turned to sponsoring excavations as a way of passing the time. His partnership with Carter led to the discovery of the tomb of Tutankh-amun, but unfortunately, he died six months after the opening of the tomb, spawning tales of a Pharaoh's curse.

Lord Carnarvon fought back, claiming that the tomb had been robbed during the reign of Ramesses IX and therefore should not be considered intact. He added that he did not want any artifacts for himself, but wanted to give pieces to the major museums of the world, especially the British Museum, the Louvre, and the Metropolitan Museum of Art. This was a shrewd move, aimed at gaining the support of these museums, foreign scholars, and politicians.

In December 1922, Carnarvon and Carter testified that the value of the artifacts was £3 million, and that Carnarvon had spent £50,000 over the course of sixteen years. James Henry Breasted volunteered as a witness that the tomb had been robbed and was not intact. But even *The Times* of London, the newspaper that had exclusive rights to the story and was clearly on Carnarvon's side, published an article stating that according to the law all the artifacts should go to the Egyptian Museum.

Eventually, however, the Egyptian government announced that the English expedition did not have the right to take any of the artifacts from the tomb. Carter insisted that the tomb was intact except for the robbery that had taken place twenty-five years after the death of Tutankhamun, and that no one had entered the tomb since 1377 B.C. Carter thought that this would give him the right to take half of the artifacts.

Stick with curved end in form of a Nubian captive A variety of styles and shapes of walking stick were found in the tomb. This beautifully carved gilded wood and ebony example sports a handle in the form of a Nubian captive.

However, the Egyptians took it as evidence against his cause because the statement meant that the tomb was essentially intact.

Carnarvon, having spent a great deal of money to find the tomb, was thinking about how he could use the tomb for his own purposes. His plan was to make a film with a Hollywood film company about the discovery, from which he would gain £20,000. He also intended to produce four popular volumes about the tomb, which he thought he could sell for £8.10s. He made a deal with The London *Times*, which he signed on January 10, 1923, that they could have exclusive rights to the story, and sell the news to other newspapers. Seventy-five percent of this money would go to *The Times*, and the other twenty-five percent was to go to Carnarvon. In fact, the paper gave Carnarvon £5,000 right away, and gave £2,500 to his widow after his death.

Both the national and the international press were angry and astonished that anyone would try to control the rights to such an important story. It turned out to be a huge mistake, and one for which Carter had to pay. It is difficult to fathom that when Egyptian reporters wanted to enter the tomb, Carter or Carnarvon would deny them access. The Egyptian press wrote to the Antiquities Service, the Egyptian government, and also to Carnarvon and Carter, expressing their outrage. Lacau wrote to Carter, asking him to permit just one visit to the tomb by the Egyptian press, but Carter, focused intensely on the recording, conservation, and clearance of the tomb and wanting as little disturbance as possible, said no. On January 26, 1923, Carter agreed finally to one visit by the press, but this was nearly not enough to assuage their indignation.

Egypt officially gained its independence on February 28, 1923, but the Egyptians did not consider this true independence, as they were still greatly under the management of the British. The nationalist press said that Egypt was not independent yet because Carter and Carnarvon represented imperialism. They controlled the tomb, which was on Egyptian land. The press went to war against Carnarvon and Carter, and began to write stories

OPPOSITE: **Folding stool** The seat of this stool, made of ebony inlaid with ivory, imitates the skin of a cow—note the tail with the ivory tuft that hangs down at one side. As is common for such furniture, the feet are in the shape of goose heads.

accusing them of being involved in stealing objects from the tomb. *The Daily Express* wrote: "If science becomes commercial then it is prostitution." Carter told the press that the Egyptians were incapable and did not know anything about scientific excavation, and that the officials cared only about politics.

But Carter and Carnarvon had made a serious mistake from the very beginning when they alienated the head of the Antiquities Service. Pierre Lacau noticed that Carter was recording the artifacts in a register at the Egyptian Museum but keeping a duplicate register at the tomb. He informed Carter that he needed the names of all of his assistants, so that he could approve or disapprove their inclusion on the team. He also insisted that no one could visit the tomb without permission from the Egyptian government. He also objected to the granting of exclusive rights to *The Times*.

In February 1923, Morcus Hana became the minister of irrigation, with the Antiquities Department under his supervision. When Carter went to see Hana to congratulate him on his new appointment, he opened a new dialogue about the tomb, hoping to get him on Carnarvon's side. But this was to prove fruitless, and Hana ended up siding with the Antiquities Service.

At one point, Carter wanted to invite a group of twenty-two ladies to visit the tomb but the Egyptian government refused. Carter was upset and sent a letter to the Egyptian government to inform them that he had decided to close the tomb. This was a mistake because once the tomb was closed, further conservation was impossible. When Carter himself went back to the tomb, he was prevented from entering by the Egyptian police. Carter, very frustrated, sent a telegram to Morcus Hana, but it was to no avail.

Carter refused to agree to with the conditions set by the government: that the division of artifacts be foregone; and that anyone who wanted to visit the tomb had first to get permission from the Egyptian government. Carter took the Egyptian government to court and asked that Lacau make a public apology. Hana stated that he made the rules, not Lacau.

Saad Zaghloul, prime minister of Egypt and the head of Wafd Party, announced in a speech in February 15, 1923 that "Mr. Carter had behaved in

OPPOSITE: King Fuad Fuad, king of Egypt, paid a state visit to the Valley of the Kings to see Howard Carter's work on the tomb.

Goose unguent container The many jars and pots for ointments included this lovely container in the shape of a trussed goose.

a way that the government cannot accept because he agreed in writing at the time of the official visit, and then did not respect his agreement."

The Egyptian people felt offended because the tomb belonged to Egypt, not to Howard Carter or Lord Carnarvon. They were also upset by Carter and Carnarvon's behavior, especially by the fact that Egyptian officials and press had been prevented from visiting the tomb. After the action of Minister Hana, many people demonstrated in the streets, saying, "Long live the Minister of Tutankhamun." The foreign press began to support Carter. They objected to the government's decision to stop Carter's work on the tomb, and talked about how important this discovery was to Egypt and the world.

On February 20, 1923, the Egyptian cabinet canceled the concession that had been given to Lord Carnarvon. They based their decision on Carter's closing of the tomb, which exposed the artifacts inside to the risk of damage and decay. The Egyptian newspaper *al-Muqattam* wrote that what had happened should

be a lesson to the Egyptians—that we should learn more about excavation and know how to study our monuments ourselves!

Carter responded by bringing two court cases against the Egyptian government and made two important requests: first, for a half share in the antiquities found in the tomb and second, for the opportunity to restore the artifacts. During this period, Carter made a statement to the press that Morcus Hanna was a thief. Many people, such as Alan Gardiner and James Breasted, tried to mediate between Carter and the Egyptian government. They met with the minister and talked to him about the importance of the conservation of the artifacts and argued that Carter should be allowed to return. Acting responsibly, the minister agreed, but with conditions. These were as follows: One, Carter should make an official apology to the Egyptians because he had used the word 'thief' in a newspaper interview. Two, Carter and Lady Carnarvon would not share in the division of the artifacts. Three, another article should be written stating that the minister

An Egyptian restorer at work

of irrigation had the right to supervise and control everything concerning the tomb.

Carter, furiously angry, was advised to leave Egypt. He decided to go to the United States for a lecture tour. His colleagues were concerned because Carter was not a good lecturer and had no formal education in Egyptology. Many people, including representatives of the Metropolitan Museum of Art in New York, met with Morcus Hana to apologize on Carter's behalf. The minister demanded that Carter himself come and apologize, but the excavator refused at first. Finally, Carter realized that the Egyptian government would never let him work in Egypt again without a public apology. He wrote a letter indicating that he would not ask for fifty percent of the artifacts and withdrew all court cases.

On December 15, 1924, Saad Zagloul resigned and Ahmed Ziwar Pasha became the prime minister of Egypt. The new prime minister met with Carter at the Automobile Club on January 4, 1925. At the meeting, Carter tried to take back the letter that he had written stating that he would not ask for fifty percent of the objects. Ziwar Pasha told Carter that the government would give Lady Carnarvon (whose husband had died in 1923) some of the duplicate artifacts, and would allow Carter to work at the tomb.

Carter arrived back in Luxor on January 25, 1925. He found that the sun had weathered the tomb, that the color of the jewelry had changed, and that the wooden artifacts had begun to deteriorate. His restorer, Alfred Lucas, had an enormous job to conserve the tomb and the artifacts. Carter, taking advantage in this case of the fact that the Egyptian government clearly owned the tomb, asked them to pay seventy-five thousand Egyptian pounds for restoration and excavation, and officially requested some of the duplicate artifacts. The battle went on for the next four years, as the objects were brought from the tomb, recorded, and carefully conserved.

In 1929, Mohamed Mahmoud Pasha, who had succeeded Ziwar Pasha as prime minister of Egypt, made the important pronouncement that henceforth Egypt could not give antiquities to individuals, only to institutions such as the British Museum; therefore, neither Carter nor Lady Carnarvon could receive any objects from the tomb. He also announced that Egypt could not take money for Egyptian artifacts.

At the end of 1929, Carter finished his recording and conservation of the tomb of Tutankhamun and terminated his formal relationship by giving the keys of the tomb to the local inspector. Carter gained a great deal of recognition through his discovery; in fact, he became the most famous archaeologist in the world. He met the president of the United States of America, and Yale University gave him an honorary degree. However, at the Egyptian Museum, where there are monuments to famous archaeologists such as Mariette and Ahmed Pasha Kamal, a tribute to Carter has never been erected. However, with all his mistakes, he made a spectacular discovery and did excellent conservation of its fabulous artifacts. Therefore, we are now planning to honor him by making his rest house at Qurna into a museum dedicated to his memory.

It has long been suspected, although never proven, that Carter and Carnarvon stole artifacts from the tomb of Tutankhamun. Their illegal maneuvering may have begun almost as soon as the tomb was discovered. There is a great deal of evidence that Carter opened and then closed a hole in the plaster blocking and entered in the company of Lord Carnarvon and Carnarvon's daughter, Evelyn, who was deeply in love with

Statues of Herwer and Duamutef Many statues were found in Tutankhamun's tomb. These one third life-size statues are of gilded wood.

Carter at the time, before the official opening of the tomb. They may even have entered the Burial Chamber, or at least looked in, at this time.

All the people who attended the official event said that Carter was very nervous; he may well have been worried that someone would notice the hole in the doorway. Lucas noticed this hole in December, and Carter evidently admitted his breach of protocol to him. Lucas mentioned once in a speech that he had seen a perfume box from the chamber at Carter's house in Luxor before the official opening of the tomb; fortunately, Carter did return this item. When Ibrahim Efendi Habieb, the local inspector of antiquities, came to the tomb for the first time, Carter and Carnarvon prevented him from entering the tomb until they had returned all the artifacts that would betray that it had been opened. Additional evidence for the unofficial entry comes from a letter sent by Lady Evelyn to Carter, which she wrote three days after entering the tomb. In the letter, she thanks him for letting her see the tomb and says that entering it at night was something that she will never forget.

Carter left Cairo in December and met with King George V of England. During the royal audience, he announced to the press that he was soon to uncover the king's mummy. How did he know that the mummy was there? This story is recorded both by Mohsen Mohamed, an Egyptian writer, and Thomas Hoving, former director of the Metropolitan Museum of Art in New York, both of whom wrote excellent books about the discovery.

Hoving provides convincing evidence in his book that Carter and Carnarvon did steal objects from the tomb, several of which are now in the Metropolitan Museum. These stolen objects include a scepter, a gold ring, a statue made of ivory, and an alabaster perfume vessel. At least four other artifacts from the tomb have been found in other museums, including a broad collar and a spoon of ivory. It is likely that these museums bought these objects from someone who had bought them from Carter's family. The beautiful head of Tutankhamun as Nefertem rising from the lotus was found by antiquities inspectors carefully wrapped and packed in a crate, sitting near the entrance

OPPOSITE: **View into Burial Chamber** Tutankhamun was buried inside a nest of golden shrines, a large stone sarcophagus, and three inner coffins. This view into the chamber was taken from the Antechamber just after the plaster blocking hiding the burial had been taken down.

to the tomb. Carter claimed that he had found it in the corridor and then wrapped it for safekeeping; but it has long been suspected that Carter was planning to steal this elegant masterpiece.

The discovery of the tomb caused no amount of trouble in many places. Even the relationship between Carter and Carnarvon became difficult, and their professional relationship was severed. Trouble began between them soon after the discovery of the tomb. Carnarvon's daughter, Lady Evelyn Herbert is thought to have fallen in love with Carter at their first meeting in Luxor on November 23, 1922. The letter that she sent to Carter soon afterward thanking him for allowing her to see the tomb contained many words that can be interpreted as evidence of the love of a young lady of twenty for a man of almost fifty. It seems, however, that Carter ignored her completely, as a result of which she may have tried to poison the relationship between Carter and her father.

According to one version of events, Lady Evelyn told Lord Carnarvon that she was in love with Carter. Carnarvon was angry and upset, appalled that she could be in love with a man who was so much older and of a lower class. Carnarvon said that he could not let her marry someone who was an employee. He went directly to Carter's tent and confronted Carter, who replied that he had no time for love. He was in love only with his work and had no interest in Lady Evelyn. The two men argued and Carter dismissed Carnarvon from his tent. Lord Carnarvon left, swearing that he would never return. Gardiner and Breasted tried to get the two men to talk again, but had no success.

This was the end of the partnership between Carter and Carnarvon. The two men never worked together again. After several months, Lord Carnarvon decided that he made a mistake and sent a letter to Carter in which he said that he had behaved the way he had because of what Evelyn had told him, but that he respected Carter as a friend and was a man who had few friends. We do not know what might have happened after this because soon afterward, Carnarvon went to Aswan, where he was bitten by a mosquito. The bite became infected, and on May 6, 1923, he died in his room at the Shepheard Hotel.

OPPOSITE: **Name jewel of Tutankhamun** This lovely object, like the winged scarab seen on page 120, is a rebus for the throne name of Tutankh-amun, Nebkheperure.

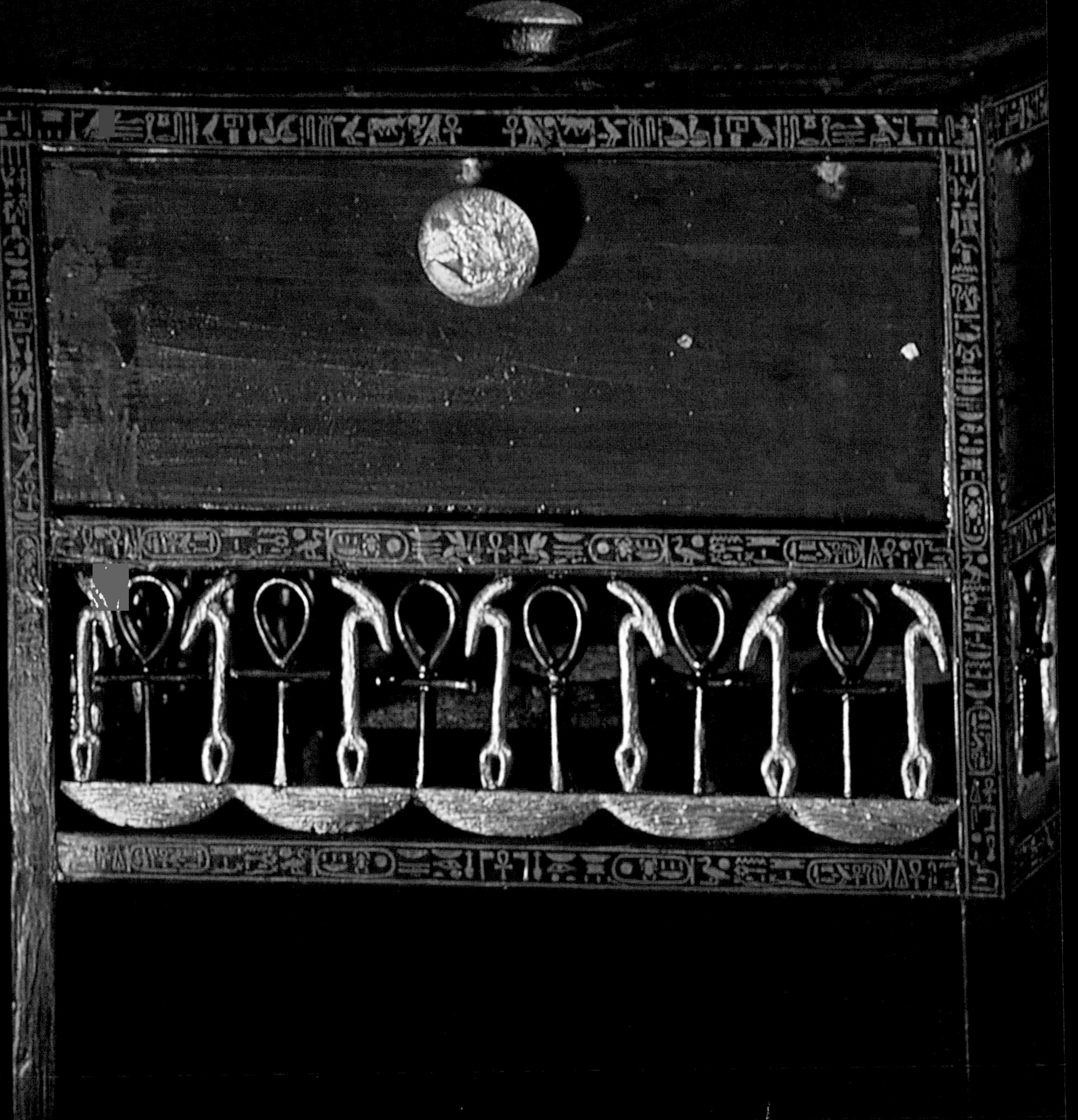

CHAPTER TWELVE

THE CURSE OF TUTANKHAMUN

THE DEATH OF LORD CARNARVON LESS THAN SIX MONTHS AFTER the opening of the tomb of Tutankhamun caused some people to believe that there was a curse attached to the tomb. Newspapers reported that his death was caused by mysterious, ominous forces unleashed from the mummy and its trappings; at least one even went so far as to mistranslate a text inscribed on a mud brick found before the Anubis shrine in the Treasury: "I will kill all of those who cross this threshold into the sacred precincts of the royal king who lives forever." In reality, this text reads: "I am the one who prevents the sand from blocking the secret chamber" (translation by David Silverman).

Carnarvon became sick while he was still in Aswan, the victim of an infection that entered his already frail body through a mosquito bite on his cheek. He was moved to Cairo for better medical care, where he died a few days later. Proponents of the curse reported that the lights in Cairo went out at the precise monument of his death. Carnarvon's son, Lord Porchester, added to the mystery by recounting that his father's dog, still at home in the family castle, Highclere, let out a pitiful cry at the moment of its master's death, and then died also.

In fact, there were no real mysteries surrounding the death of Carnarvon. He died of blood poisoning triggered by the infected mosquito bite, which he had cut open with his razor while shaving. The lights in Cairo may well

OPPOSITE: **Wooden chest from the tomb of Tutankhamun** RIGHT: **The goddess Selket** This statue, seen in situ in the photograph on page 147, protects the canopic shrine of Tutankhamun.

have gone off when Carnarvon died, but this would not have been an unusual occurrence, since the electrical system in Egypt was extremely unreliable at the time. We have no independent witnesses to the case of the dog, and it is interesting to note that Carnarvon's son was himself in India at the time.

But the curse was born, and soon acquired a life of its own. Newspaper reporters attributed every accident or death possible to it. Anyone who had visited the tomb and then died anytime soon (including one man who fell while entering the tomb and later died of his injuries) was said to be a victim of the curse. An Egyptian prince living in London, who had nothing to do with Tutankhamun and had never been to the tomb, murdered his wife; he was said to have been affected by the curse. Even the early death at forty-two of Jean-François Champollion, the man who deciphered hieroglyphs, was put down to the curse of the pharaohs, notwithstanding the fact that Champollion died in 1832, almost a hundred years before Tutankhamun came to light. In fact, the mortality rate of the people most closely associated with the tomb was very low. Arthur Mace died in 1928, but he had been sickly for a long time. Carter himself lived until 1939; Breasted died in 1935; Lucas died in 1945; Gardiner lived until 1963; and Lady Evelyn died in 1980 at the age of seventy-nine.

The curse of the pharaohs has had a very long life. A German journalist wrote a popular book called *Curse of the Pharaohs* in the 1970s, five decades after the death of Carnarvon. In this sensationalist tale, he reports that he met Gamal Mehrez, then director of antiquities, at the Omar El Khayyam Hotel in Cairo and asked him, "Do you believe in the curse?" Mehrez said, "I have excavated tombs and mummies and nothing has ever happened to me." According the author of this book, Mehrez died the next day.

It is easy when you hear a story like this to believe in the curse. But what most people do not know was that Gamal Mehrez specialized in Islamic archaeology and had never excavated anything related to pharaonic Egypt. Also, Mehrez had serious health problems. What happened to him was a coincidence and not a curse.

OPPOSITE: **Shrine of Anubis** This image of the mortuary god Anubis, the deity responsible for the preparation of the mummy, stood in the entrance to the Treasury. This small room to the north of the Burial Chamber held the canopic material of the king, along with many wonderful statues and a great deal of jewelry.

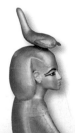

Other accidents and deaths have been attributed to the curse. When Egyptian President Nasser issued a decree that the objects of Tutankhamun were to travel to France, an archaeologist named Mohamed Ibrahim objected, and later was hit by a car. The director of antiquities, Mohammed Mahdy, signed a contract agreeing that Tutankhamun's objects would travel to London; he was killed while crossing a busy street. Judging from these two deaths, the curse could not decide whether or not the treasures of Tutankhamun should leave the country.

Ancient Egyptians did leave inscriptions warning passersby not to do harm to their tombs. Most of ancient Egyptian curses are couched in the form of threats, and occur mainly on the monuments of private citizens, mainly of the Old Kingdom, rather than of royalty. Here is an example of a private curse:

As for any one who will do something
*   evil against my grave*
Seize a stone from this my tomb
Remove any stone or any brick from this
*   my tomb*
Enter my tomb
Enter this tomb in impurity
Enter upon these my images in impurity

He will be judged regarding it by the
*   great god*
I will wring his neck like a bird and
*   cause those*
who live upon earth to fear the spirits
*   who are in the west*
I will exterminate his survivors.
I will not allow their forms to be occupied.

Another inscription is one that turned up in the excavations of the Upper Cemetery of the Tomb of the Pyramid Builders at Giza. In the tomb of an artist named Petety was found the following inscription:

O all people who enter this tomb,
Who will make evil against this tomb and destroy it:
May the crocodile be against them on water,
And snakes against them on land.
May the hippopotamus against them on water,
The scorpion against them on land.

David Silverman, currently curator in charge of the Egyptian Section at the University Museum, University of Pennsyl-vania, observed in an article on the

so-called curse of the pharaohs that the
dearth of royal curses might indicate
that royalty had other protection against
its enemies. Royal curses, when they do
occur, are directed more toward this life
than the next. For example, there is an
address in the mortuary temple of
Hatshepsut at Deir al-Bahari, in which
Thutmosis I, in speaking of his daughter, proclaims: "He who will adore her
he will live, he who will speak evil in a
curse against her majesty, he will die."

As a young archaeologist, I participated in excavations at the site of Kom
Abu Billo in the Nile Delta. At the end
of my first season, I was responsible
for taking the artifacts from the excavations (mostly of Greco-Roman
tombs) to the Egyptian Museum in
Cairo. That same day, my aunt died.
The second year, on the day when I moved the artifacts, my uncle died, and
the third year it was my favorite cousin. Newspapers in Cairo reported that
these things happened because of the curse. But the truth is that there is no
'curse of the pharaohs.' Even the ancient Egyptians, when they inscribed curses on their tombs, only hoped that the words would protect their burials.

Most of the people whose deaths were associated with the 'curse' were foreigners who had nothing to do with the excavation of the tomb. Only one person
who was related to the discovery died at the time, and that was Lord Carnarvon.

After seventy-five years the phrase 'curse of the pharaohs' still fascinates the
public and Hollywood producers. Fortunately, there is really no such thing.

ABOVE: **Curse of Petety** Recent excavations in the Cemetery of the Pyramid Builders at Giza uncovered
this inscription in the tomb of a minor official named Petety and his wife, Nesyhor. The curse threatens
those that might disturb the tomb with snakes, hippos, lions, and crocodiles. FOLLOWING PAGES: **Painted
floor from Amarna**

CONCLUSION

CHAPTER THIRTEEN

THE TRAVELS OF TUTANKHAMUN

MANY OBJECTS FROM THE TOMB OF THE TUTANKHAMUN HAVE traveled from Cairo to museums in Europe, Russia, Canada, Japan, and the United States. The first time that objects from the Tutankhamun collection left Egypt was in 1961 to go to the United States, where they stayed until January 1964, touring about seventeen cities. The same objects traveled to Canada from 1965 to 1966. After that, the tour went to Japan and France, where they were on exhibit from 1965 to 1967. This tour did a great deal for relations between Egypt and all of these countries, especially Japan, whose emperor was very impressed by the artifacts.

From 1973 until 1975 a new exhibit went to England and to the Soviet Union, where the Soviet minister of culture and Gamal Mokhtar, head of the Egyptian Antiquities Organization, opened the exhibit together. That same year, the United States asked that fifty objects from the Tutankhamun collection be allowed to visit six cities in the States as well as Toronto in Canada. A seventh U.S. city was added later so that the city of San Francisco could also host the golden king. The opening was in September 1976 in Washington D.C.; President Nixon was expected to attend, but Henry Kissinger came instead. When Jimmy Carter became the U.S. president, his daughter, Amy, came to see the exhibit. The director of the Cairo Museum, Ibrahim el Nawawy, explained the exhibit to her, and she was so impressed with the magnificence of Tutankhamun's artifacts that she told her father. Afterwards, the president invited el Nawawy to give a lecture at the White House.

OPPOSITE: **Two shabtis of Tutankhamun**

In Germany, the curse of Tutankhamun really happened. The statue of Selket, one of the gilded wooden goddesses who protected the shrine in which the young king lay was dropped. The shoulder and the head were damaged, and the royal uraeus that adorned her head was broken. Fortunately, a conservator from America was able to repair the statue and bring it back to its original form. But the damage had already been done, and when the objects returned to Egypt in 1981, Egyptian journalists wrote stories arguing against sending artifacts outside of Egypt. The Egyptian parliament convened and decided that Tutankhamun's artifacts would not travel outside Egypt again. I am glad that, after two decades, the Swiss have persuaded us to let Tutankhamun again visit the world.

The rocky hills of Thebes still hide more secrets. Since the discovery of Tutankhamun, only two major discoveries have been made: an enormous cache of statues found in the temple of Luxor, and the rediscovery of KV5, the tomb of the sons of Ramesses II. Some of the New Kingdom kings are still missing, so it is possible that another cache of royal mummies will be found. There are also tombs found in the last century and a half that have not yet been properly recorded. There is still much work to do in the Valley of the Kings before we can say that we have solved all its mysteries.

OPPOSITE: **The golden throne of Tutankhamun on display in the Egyptian Museum in Cairo.**

TUTANKHAMUN
REDISCOVERED

In 2002, THE EGYPTIAN MUSEUM IN CAIRO CELEBRATED ITS CENTENNIAL. To mark this important event, the museum mounted a new exhibit called "Hidden Treasures of the Egyptian Museum." At the instigation of Dr. Nadia Loutka, chief conservator at the museum, curators went through some of the packed storerooms in the museum basement, and brought some of the treasures that were found hidden away out for display.

Among the objects still in the basement are a number of pieces from the tomb of Tutankhamun. Several of these have never been displayed, and have only been published in scholarly contexts. I have chosen six of these pieces, fragments of gold foil once attached to chariots or horse trappings, to illustrate and describe here.

Six complete but dismantled chariots were found in Tutankhamun's tomb, four stacked in the Antechamber and the other two in the Treasury. Since the axles were too wide to fit through the entrance corridor, the workers and priests responsible for the burial had taken them apart in order to get them into the tomb. Further damage had been done by the robbers who violated the tomb, who stripped them of some of the small pieces of gold that adorned them; the priests who cleaned up after the thieves had simply piled them up, so that Carter and his team discovered them in tangled heaps. Many hours of patient excavation and preservation work allowed five of the six chariots to be reconstructed and displayed.

Along with the chariots were harnesses for horses, quivers, bow cases, and the like. The fragments of gold foil shown here were attached to a backing of

OPPOSITE: **Alabaster vases in the Antechamber**

leather, and would have been used to decorate harnesses, other parts of chariots or other weapons. Because of the fragmentary nature of the preserved leather, it is often hard to determine which specific objects these pieces of gold once adorned.

We know from depictions in Egyptian art and descriptions on monuments that Egyptian kings used chariots, first introduced to Egypt by the Hyksos in the seventeenth century B.C., for war, hunting, and royal processions. The first Egyptian text to mention a chariot is a stele of King Kamose, one of the warrior kings of Thebes who fought against the Hyksos. Pharaohs are often seen in battle scenes, for example on the pylons of temples, dominating the battlefield from their chariots. These lightweight, highly maneuverable military vehicles could be given as royal gifts, and kings are known to have inquired after the welfare of the chariot horses of their allies. These appliqués, all of which were found in the antechamber, bear images of hunting and war, appropriate for objects associated with the chariots and horses that were used for these endeavors.

Chariots of Tutankhamun Four chariots were found in the Antechamber of the tomb, stacked in a tangled heap.

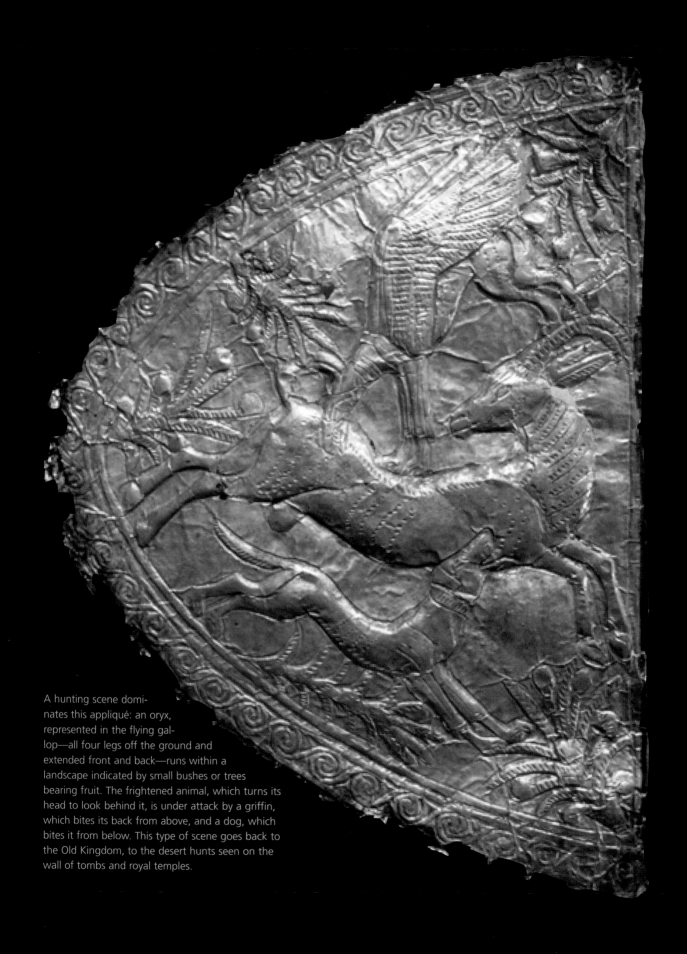

A hunting scene dominates this appliqué: an oryx, represented in the flying gallop—all four legs off the ground and extended front and back—runs within a landscape indicated by small bushes or trees bearing fruit. The frightened animal, which turns its head to look behind it, is under attack by a griffin, which bites its back from above, and a dog, which bites it from below. This type of scene goes back to the Old Kingdom, to the desert hunts seen on the wall of tombs and royal temples.

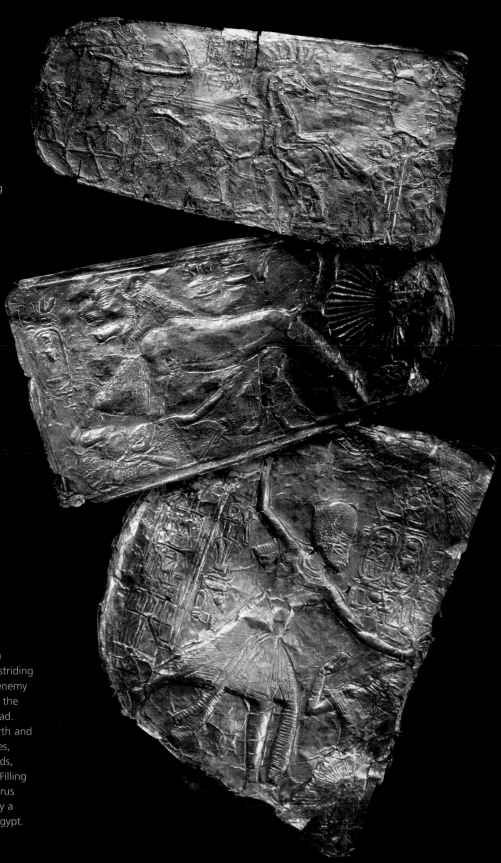

On the face of this gold fragment is an image of the king in his chariot, which is drawn by two plumed horses. The king shoots an arrow at a target whose shape identifies it as a bronze ingot, probably imported from Cyprus; it has already been penetrated by five arrows. Tutankhamun's great-great-grandfather was renowned for his prowess at archery, including his ability to shoot arrows through a thick target while driving his own chariot, just as Tutankhamun is depicted doing here.

This gold piece shows the king as a sphinx, roaring as he tramples an Asiatic enemy, who squirms beneath his paws. In front of the sphinx is the king's name, "King of Upper and Lower Egypt, Nebkheperure, given life," and above his back is written: "Trampling all the foreign lands."

This semi-circular appliqué bears an image of the king in a flowing kilt striding forward, grasping an unidentified enemy by the hair in order to kill him with the scimitar that he raises above his head. Before the king are inscribed his birth and throne names: "Lord of appearances, Tutankhamun, Lord of the Two Lands, Nebkheperure, given life like Re." Filling the space behind the king is his Horus name. The king is protected here by a vulture, patron goddess of Upper Egypt.

In this piece, the king drives his war chariot pulled by plumed horses over the prostrate body of an enemy. He wears his blue war crown and elaborate robes. Before him is an inscription that reads: "Trampling all the foreign lands," and above his head is his throne name: "Nebkheperure, given life."

This fragment depicts Tutankhamun, wearing the blue war crown, grasping a fallen enemy by the hair with one hand and a large mace with the other. His costume is an elaborate pleated kilt that flows to his ankles, a floral collar, chest bands, and ribbons. The queen, identified as "great royal wife, his beloved, mistress of the Two Lands, Ankhsenamun," stands behind him. The inscription before the king reads: "Lord of ritual, Nebkheperure, given life like Re forever."

BIBLIOGRAPHY AND SUGGESTED READING

Freed, Rita E., *et al.*, eds. *Pharaohs of the Sun*. Italy: Bullfinch Press, 1999.

Hawass, Zahi. *Silent Images: Women in Pharaonic Egypt*. Cairo: The American University in Cairo Press, and New York: Harry N. Abrams, 2000.

Kozloff, Arielle and Betsy Bryan. *Egypt's Dazzling Sun*. Bloomington: Indiana University Press, 1992.

Lichtheim, Miriam. *Ancient Egyptian Literature: A Book of Readings*. Berkeley and Los Angeles: University of California Press, 1976.

Redford, Donald B. *The Oxford Encyclopedia of Ancient Egypt*. Cairo: The American University in Cairo Press, and Oxford: Oxford University Press, 2001.

Reeves, Nicholas. *The Complete Tutankhamun: The King, the Tomb, the Royal Treasures*. Cairo: The American University in Cairo Press, and London: Thames and Hudson, 1990.

Reeves, Nicholas and Richard H. Wilkinson. *The Complete Valley of the Kings: Tombs and Treasures of Egypt's Greatest Pharaohs*. Cairo: The American University in Cairo Press, and London: Thames and Hudson, 1996.

Shaw, Ian. *The Oxford History of Ancient Egypt*. Oxford: Oxford University Press, 2000.